*TRAINING IN INDEXING*
*A Course of the Society of Indexers*

# TRAINING IN INDEXING

*A Course of the Society of Indexers*

edited by G. Norman Knight

THE M.I.T. PRESS

*Massachusetts Institute of Technology*
*Cambridge, Massachusetts, and London, England*

# CONTRIBUTORS

Eric James Coates, F.L.A. Editor, *The British Technology Index*

Robert Louis Collison, F.L.A. former Librarian, British Broadcasting Corporation, Head, Reference Department, University Research Library, University of California, Los Angeles. Author of *Indexes and Indexing* and *Indexing Books*

Peter Ferriday, B.A., F.L.A. former Editor, *British Humanities Index*

Arthur Reginald Hewitt, F.L.A. Librarian and Curator, Freemasons' Hall, London. Indexer-in-Chief of Halsbury's *Statutes of England* (26 Vols.) and *Laws of England* (42 Vols.)

J. Edwin Holmstrom, B.Sc. (Eng.) Ph.D. Free-lance technical translator, writer, and indexer

Leonard Charles Johnson, J.P., F.R.S.A. Before retirement, the first archivist, British Transport Commission

Gilfred Norman Knight, M.A. Barrister-at-Law. Founder and former Chairman (now a Vice-President) of the Society of Indexers. Wheatley Medallist for outstanding index of 1967

Derek W. Langridge, B.A., Dip.Ed., A.L.A. Principal Lecturer, School of Librarianship, North-Western Polytechnic, London

Brigadier Eric Earle G. L. Searight, C.B.E., M.C. Indexer-in-Chief, *Keesing's Contemporary Archives*

James Cholmondeley Thornton, M.A. President of the Society of Indexers. Indexer of the Centenary Edition of the *Complete Works of William Hazlitt,* 21 Vols. (1930–1934) and of The Pilgrim Edition of the *Letters of Charles Dickens,* 11 Vols. (1965–     )

John Leonard Thornton, F.L.A. Librarian, St. Bartholomew's Hospital Medical College, London, former Editor of *The Indexer.* Has indexed many medical works.

# CONTENTS

# EDITOR'S INTRODUCTION

G. NORMAN KNIGHT

A wise American writer once remarked that "the presence of an index means that the author and publisher respect the book and that a reader will respect it." A book or periodical without an index has been likened to a country without a map, and it is now generally accepted that nearly every work of nonfiction is far more useful if provided with such a chart in the form of an index. It is also certainly arguable that new editions of classical novels (e.g., *Don Quixote*) would be greatly improved by the inclusion of indexes.[1]

This being so, the question arises: How is the indexer to acquire the necessary skill? To compile a simple list of items in alphabetical order may need no great measure of expert ability, although even here some knowledge of the technique is desirable. Nothing, one imagines, could be easier than to index a collection of hymns, and yet the index to a certain hymnbook contains this somewhat startling entry:

> O Lord, what boots, 87

On hastening to page 87 the reader is reassured by finding that the actual first lines are:

> O Lord, what boots it to recall
> The hours of anguish spent

[1] Dr. Johnson urged his friend Samuel Richardson to produce an *index rerum* to his novels, and the latter did in fact publish a 450-page volume containing solely such indexes to *Pamela, Clarissa,* and *Sir Charles Grandison.*

A similarly fatuous entry has recently been brought to light in the index to Ira D. Sankey's *Sacred Songs and Solos* (1873):

> There is a land mine

whereas the hymn in fact begins:

> There is a land mine eyes hath seen

What a transformation might have been made in both instances by the mere addition of three words to the index heading!

On each side of the Atlantic exist textbooks on the subject of indexing, to be studied or consulted, but the number is inconsiderable. A brief bibliography which may prove helpful is provided at the end of this volume.

Such manuals are not many in number and they vary in quality, but they are there for the instruction of the potential indexer. There are other means of acquiring the necessary expertness, one of which is the hard way: learning by experimenting from scratch—by trial and error. Some of us who adopted this method many years ago feel a certain sense of shame when we glance again at our earliest untutored efforts. A far more satisfactory method is to study thoroughly the indexing masterpieces and to note the principles used in them. Among these must be reckoned: Wheatley's index to *Pepys's Diary* (1893–1899); Esmund de Beer's index to *Evelyn's Diary* (1955); and the Yale edition of the series based upon Boswell's *Journal*; or again, in the world of science, E. J. Coates's annual *British Technology Index* and the indexes to the American *Chemical Abstracts*.

But of what is probably the most useful means of all, oral instruction in the art of indexing, there was none in Great Britain, so far as can be discovered, until the newly formed Society of Indexers started a training course in April, 1958. It is true that every year between 1933 and 1945 the (British) Library Association used to set as part of its final examination a three-hour paper equally divided between questions on indexing and on abstracting. But there were no evening classes or training courses in connection with this paper, which was abandoned in 1945.

In the United States it has been otherwise. Already by about the turn of the half-century John Askling was lecturing on indexing at the Universities of Denver, Colorado, and of Southern California, and at Columbia University, New York.[2] It is noteworthy that more recently, when he accepted an appointment to teach "Literature in the English language" at a school in Salisbury, Connecticut, he straightway introduced indexing and abstracting into the curriculum. May this pioneer effort be widely followed!

The Society of Indexers' first training course, which was confined to its own members, was held at the School of Librarianship of University College, London University. There were six lecturers, two of whom (Robert Collison and Norman Knight) are represented by contributions to the present volume. A particularly valuable feature of those talks was found to be the discussions and sharing of experience that followed them, and from these stemmed the discussion meetings that are still held regularly—normally four a year—as part of the Society's activities.

Since those early days five further courses have been held by the Society, all at the North-Western Polytechnic, Camden Town, London. Attendance is open to all, but a modest fee is charged. There is no lack of applicants. These more recent talks at the Polytechnic comprise the succeeding chapters. Aslib (the Association of Special Libraries and Information Bureaux) of London has also been active in promoting oral instruction. In January, 1961, it arranged, jointly with the Society of Indexers, a highly successful one-day conference on better indexes for technical literature, a conference attended by 130 persons. The first

[2] In the summer of 1966 Professor Theodore C. Hines lectured on "Indexing" in the School of Library Service of Columbia University, and New York University has conducted at least one course in this subject during the past few years. Similar instruction may be provided by other United States universities.

speaker entitled his talk "Moans of a User." Then a representative of the Cambridge University Press presented the publisher's point of view. He was followed by two members of the Society who very ably described the techniques of indexing technical books and periodicals, respectively. Each paper was followed by a well-informed discussion. Three years later Aslib provided a well-organized and most rewarding three-day course on indexing.

Who, it may be asked, are the indexers for whose qualification as such the instruction is designed? In the matter of indexing books and periodicals they may be divided into three kinds: the author-indexer, the permanently employed professional indexer, and the free-lance professional. At present an author himself receives no specific payment for his indexing services, and so can be disregarded; otherwise the classification just given takes no account of anyone who is "blockhead" enough (in the Johnsonian sense)[3] to compile an index except for money.

Books indexed by their authors are frequently encountered in both the United States and Great Britain. According to Robert J. Palmer, in the United States "the majority of scholarly books are indexed by the author."[4] This may be because the latter feels that his book will be completed most satisfactorily if he himself compiles its index. Not so long ago a controversy arose as to whether in fact the author is in every case the best indexer of his own works. It was argued that owing to his detailed knowledge of the book's contents he may be unable to see the trees for the wood and so fail to select the entries sought by the index-user. Against this contention one must remember that the first three of the Library Association's annually awarded Wheatley gold medals for outstanding indexes were won by author-indexers. It has been suggested that in this respect authors may have an unfair advantage over professional rivals in that they are able to claim almost unlimited space for their indexes. Be

[3] "Sir," said Johnson, "no man but a blockhead ever wrote except for money."—*Boswell's Life* (1776), Vol. VI, Chap. iii.
[4] "Book Indexing in the United States," *The Indexer*, Vol. 5, No. 2.

that as it may, some of the best indexes to books have been produced by their authors—and some of the worst. The truth would seem to be that, *provided he is willing to master the technique*, the author can be the ideal indexer of his own works.

Another reason for the frequency of author-compiled indexes must surely be that many a publisher includes in his standard contract a clause requiring the author, if called upon, to provide an index. It is when the agreement between publisher and author contains no such clause or else when the author, although called upon to supply an index, feels either disinclined or unqualified to compile it himself, that the professional indexer comes into his own. In his survey of American indexing already cited, Palmer states: "Estimates by editors of trade-book houses [5] of the percentage of their books that are indexed by professional indexers range from seventy to ninety per cent, while two editors of university presses report that 'five per cent' or 'a handful' of their books are indexed by professional indexers. Reports from editors of textbooks and scientific books fall between these two extremes."

Earlier it was stated that some indexers of books and periodicals are permanently employed. This is because the publishers of certain publications, including legal works, the larger encyclopedias, the *London Gazette*, *The Times* (London), post office guides and directories, and *Keesing's Contemporary Archives*, find it necessary to retain an indexing staff of one or more persons. Exact figures are lacking, but the total number of British indexers so engaged cannot be very considerable. In the United States, on the other hand, the majority of indexers today are permanent employees of their organizations. All the scientific and financial services, all the major information libraries, all the major periodical indexes and indexing services are staffed with permanent indexing personnel—and often understaffed. Such indexers

[5] A trade book is "a book intended for general readership . . . not a juvenile, not a textbook, not a technical treatise, but the sort of thing that could . . . interest everybody." (Webster)

are usually trained on the job, and provided with constant supervision, with manuals and strict vocabulary controls, and with occasional supplementary lectures. American free-lance indexing is now practically confined to books and other monographic works, and special projects.

In Britain the free-lance indexers form the great bulk of the professionals. Some may devote their whole working day to indexing for various authors and publishers, and some may combine indexing with other literary activities, while others quite frequently are engaged full-time on other work and use their spare time for their indexing, which they regard as a side line, although an important one. The distinguishing mark of the free-lance indexer is that he (or she) normally performs the tasks in his or her own home and in complete seclusion. Rightly does Collison describe free-lance indexing as "a cottage industry." It is a fact that prior to the formation of the Society of Indexers the present editor, although he had then been indexing books and periodicals for over thirty years, had not met, and did not even know the name of, a single other person operating in this field.

There are, however, certain exceptional cases on both sides of the Atlantic where the free-lance professional has set up his own business or indexing agency, in which he may include such services as proofreading and translation. In this business he will employ other free-lance indexers as well as translators etc., as the demand arises.

The chapters that follow were originally lectures delivered to an audience of English students by experts in their respective fields. This accounts for the many allusions to British practice. The lectures were intended to be in the main fairly elementary, if not exactly a "beginner's course," and to commend themselves to students with little or no practical experience. At the same time much of the information and many of the hints provided may be found profitable by the advanced indexer.

Differences in the style of the various chapters arise from the fact that four of the lectures, Chapters 1 and 2

(Robert Collison), Chapter 5 (Derek Langridge), and Chapter 8 (J. E. Holmstrom) were delivered extempore and not from prepared scripts; consequently—and this should be noted—the versions printed here were taken from edited tape recordings. Not every lecture lent itself to a practical exercise, but such exercises will be found at the end of Chapters 2, 3, 4, and 13, and the suggested solutions form the concluding pages of the book (including the index).

Regretfully the final lecture of the course, "The Indexing of Current Business Records," has had to be omitted. Delivered by the Central Registry Superintendent of a very large industrial concern, it dealt mainly with the methods and practices adopted by that company; and permission to reproduce the material has not been forthcoming. Cordial thanks are due to the actual contributors for their friendly cooperation at all stages of the book's production.

There may seem to be one or two inconsistencies in the following pages, but these are more apparent than real. Thus, Holmstrom (p. 113) points to certain differences between the indexing of scientific works and that of general titles, whereas E. J. Coates states on page 128 that there are no *fundamental* differences. But both authors agree that such differences as may exist are of degree only. Again, there is no real contradiction as to the role of classification in indexing, since Langridge, who recommends it, is referring to the preliminary classification of his subjects before getting down to their alphabetical arrangement, while Holmstrom, who decries it, is discussing the applicability of cataloguing classification to indexing.

But, as Alexander Pope wrote:

"Who shall decide when doctors disagree?"[6]

In the event of any *actual* disagreement in this volume, the discriminating reader will need to decide the issue for himself.

[6] *Moral Essays*, Epistle iii.

Finally, although, as will be seen, there are certain accepted rules in indexing, these may have to give way in exceptional cases. Common sense should prevail over all rules.

## Special Note

To American readers who have been indexing professionally for some time, much in these chapters may seem unduly elementary. We hope that they will recognize, however, that others who may be beginning their indexing careers can profit from just such instruction. This could include a large number of Britishers for whom the lectures were originally intended.

British readers are asked to be indulgent with the American publishers who have taken the liberty of substituting American spelling for the British.

## Acknowledgments

The editor is grateful to

(a) the British Standards Institution for permission to reproduce certain definitions and examples taken from B.S. 3700:1964. This pamphlet, *Recommendations for the Preparation of Indexes*, may be obtained from The British Standards Institution, 2 Park Street, London, W.1, or in the United States from the American Standards Association, Inc., 10 East 40th Street, New York, N.Y. 10016.

(b) Associated Iliffe Press Ltd., of London, W.C.1, for permission to reproduce on pages 122–123 five lines from *Eddy Currents*, published by them and SNT1, Prague, in 1967.

# DEFINITIONS OF INDEXING TERMS

ANALYTICAL INDEX. One that by means of subheadings
classifies the concepts contained in its subject entries
in accordance with the text.

COMPOUND HEADING. "A heading comprising two or more
elements (with or without connecting hyphen), each of
which could stand alone with its own meaning."[1]
Examples:
    Air-sea rescue    John o'Groat's
    Henry VIII         Underwater-to-air missiles

CROSS REFERENCE. "A direction from one heading (or any
of its subheadings) to another heading."

CUMULATIVE INDEX. Where a book is published in several
volumes, each with its own index, or where a periodical
is provided with an index each year or part of a year,
and these separate indexes are combined to form an
index to a/the whole series, the product is called a
cumulative index.

[1] The definitions in quotation marks are taken by permission from
British Standard 3700:1964—*Recommendations for the Preparation of Indexes*
pp. 6, 7.

[N.B. The index to the final volume or the last collection of periodicals will often not appear separately but will be merged in the cumulative index.]

ENTRY.[2]  "A unit of the index consisting of a heading (and qualifying expression, if any) with at least one reference to the location of the item in the text (or else with a 'See' cross-reference)," together with any subheadings and their relevant references.[3]
The presence of subheadings, when references are numerous enough for systematic grouping, constitutes a COMPLEX ENTRY.

HEADING.  "The word(s) or symbol(s) selected from, or based on, an item in the text, arranged in alphabetical or other chosen order." Examples:
Electronic computers (and other calculating devices)
*ff* (*fortissimo*)
Nelson, Lord

INDEX.  "An index is an indicator or pointer out of the position of required information"—Henry B. Wheatley, *What is an Index?* (1878).
"A systematic guide to the text of any reading matter or to the contents of other collected documentary material, comprising a series of entries, with headings arranged in alphabetical or other chosen order and with references to show where each item indexed is located."

INDEXING.  (*noun*): The compilation of an index.
(*adjective*): Pertaining to such a compilation.

INVERSION.  A compound heading (or subheading) is said to be *inverted* when the actual order of its elements is

[2] In the succeeding pages the expression "entry" or "entries" is occasionally used loosely to denote anything entered on an index card or slip.
[3] Such indexes as those on punched cards may not have entries in this sense.

reversed, in order that the second part may supply the key word. Thus:

Donne, Dean John
Drug addiction, teen-age

KEY WORD. The initial word of a heading or of a sub-heading (provided the subheadings are arranged alphabetically).

LETTER-BY-LETTER. (adjectival): The less common (*see* Word-by-Word) method, by treating the groups as single entities alphabetized all through, letter-by-letter. Examples:

North Carolina
North-easter (wind)
Northfield, Vermont
North Pole
Northumbria
North Vernon, Indiana

LINE-BY-LINE SUBHEADINGS. Subheadings arranged in columnar form under the heading. Example:

Churches
    abbey, *see* Abbey Church
    basilican
    circular
    collegiate
    cruciform plan of

MAIN HEADING. "A description sometimes used (for a heading) in contradistinction to subheading."

*Passim.* Used after a sequence of page references (e.g., 45–49 *passim*), it denotes that the subject of the heading or subheading is referred to not continuously, but in scattered passages, throughout those pages of the text.

QUALIFIED HEADING. A simple or compound heading is said to be qualified when descriptive words are added, following punctuation or parenthesis. Examples (qualifying words here in *italics*):

Henry VII (*first Tudor king*)

Henry VIII, *monasteries plundered by*

The second instance is sometimes described as MODIFICATION.

REFERENCE. The number of the page, folio, section, or paragraph, or other specific indication where the item or subject indexed is to be found in the text.

RUN-ON SUBHEADINGS. Subheadings arranged to follow one another in ordinary paragraph form and spread over the entire column. Example:

Churches: abbey, *see* Abbey Church; basilican, 258–263, 308; circular, 305, 390; collegiate, 402; cruciform plan of, 319, 375; English medieval, 390, 489; French Gothic, 530, 542; Georgian, 949–955

*See* CROSS REFERENCE. "A direction from one heading (or subheading), after which there are no page or other references, to an alternative heading, under which all the relevant references to an item in the text are collected."

*See also* CROSS REFERENCE. "A direction from one heading (or subheading) to any additional heading(s), under which further relevant references to an item in the text are to be found." Example:

Churches:

Roman (*see also* Constantine), 273–275

Romanesque (*see also* Orders, religious, *and* Romanesque Revival), 309, 324, 542

This usage is preferred by the *American Standard Basic Criteria for Indexes*; but the Chicago *Manual of Style* uses the following form.

Churches

Roman, 273–275. *See also* Constantine

Romanesque, 309, 324, 542. *See also* Orders, religious, *and* Romanesque Revival

SIMPLE HEADING. "A heading consisting of a single word or a word with a hyphened prefix . . . or suffix which alone would either have no meaning or have a different meaning." Examples:

| | | |
|---|---|---|
| Nonage | Pickling | Standards |
| Non-aged | Pick-me-ups | Stand-by |
| Nonagenarians | Pick-ups | Stand-in |
| Non-barking dogs | Picnics | Standings |

[The examples given here refer to British usage. Many words hyphened in Britain are not so treated in the United States.]

SUBHEADING. "The word(s) or symbol(s) under which references in a complex entry are specifically located." Example:

| | |
|---|---|
| Nelson, Lord | (heading) |
| naval career | (subheading) |
| promotion to Admiral | (sub-subheading) |

SUBJECT- Defined in the *American Standard Basic Criteria for Indexes* (1959) as a unit concept found in, or derived from, the material indexed. The unit concept may be found or expressed as a thematic topic, a name, a date, the first line of a poem, the title of a work, an expression coined to give the gist of the material indexed, and so on.

TEXT. All the reading matter in a book (and its illustrations) other than its index.

WORD-BY-WORD. (adjectival): The more common method (*See* Letter-by-Letter) used in the alphabetical arrangement of compound headings and compound subheadings, by treating them as separate words, each alphabetized in turn. Examples:

North Carolina
North Pole
North Vernon, Indiana
North-easter (wind)
Northfield, Vermont
Northumbria

# 1

# THE ELEMENTS OF BOOK INDEXING, PART I

ROBERT L. COLLISON

The trouble with indexing is that even today we are still at the elementary stage of learning how to do it. We do not know enough about its technique. All our indexes are at sixes and sevens. No really universally accepted common rules exist on which we all agree, and each one thinks he knows better than anyone else how an index should be arranged and what should go into it. We have all had the experience, for example, of using the telephone directory and failing to find in it somebody whom we knew to exist, whom we knew to have a telephone, and who we believe has paid his account up to date. Why do we fail to find him? In some cases because his name, for some reason or other, does not appear in the telephone directory. But, many other times, it is because we have not understood the basis on which the entries in the telephone directory are arranged. In the first place, no introduction in the telephone directory explains what these rules are. You are assumed, somehow or other, to know them instinctively. And one test of this is that even if you can use the London, Glasgow, Birmingham, Hull, or any other telephone directory very skillfully indeed and never miss anything, you have difficulty, when you go abroad to other countries, in locating someone in one of their telephone directories, because these work on a different system again. One needs only to refer to the case of New York City where any good Scotsman

Copyright © 1968 by Robert L. Collison.

will be amazed to find that the names beginning with Mac and so on—to give only one very small example—are alphabetized in an entirely different way from that in Britain. One would have thought that in these days when we standardize screws and nails and all kinds of other objects that we might have reached some kind of standardization on this, but so far we have not achieved very much. There have been movements toward it, but there is trouble in getting general acceptance of them.

Now this is a very worrisome thing, because there is no doubt that without indexes our books are not properly finished. In Britain people have almost become used to a book without an index, or, if it has a so-called index, with a very insufficient and incomplete one, or in fact a thoroughly bad one. This is just taken for granted. The writer has in mind recent books, such as those theatrical autobiographies where an actress in a kind of euphoria dashes back wildly over forty years of opening nights and, for each show she was in, mentions the names of forty or fifty different people. Then when the book has appeared, A meets B in the street and says to B, "I see you got a very good write-up in Stella's new book." B, not wishing to buy the book, dashes to his nearest library and searches feverishly for this mention of his name. Two hundred and fifty pages later he emerges to track down A and tell him, "I failed to find my name, even though there is an index." So, after lunch in the nearest hostelry, they go back to the library to search the book together, A swearing that he has seen B's name. What happens? In the end they find a glowing reference to B in the preface, of all places, and a part of the volume that the indexer did not index. The fact that in the body of the book, the mention of B on page 61 is incorrectly indexed as on page 62, does not matter so much; the worst crime is that the indexer omitted to index part of the book. Now, this is a very trivial example. B's exasperation does not really matter to us a great deal, although it could be serious. At a Board Meeting, for example, one member mentions that he has seen a picture of a piece of machinery that the Board is considering buying. Everybody on the Board agrees that it would be a thoroughly good idea if they could have a look at this picture. It would help them in their deliberations. And what happens? The picture certainly does not turn up at the Board Meeting because pictures in advertisements are not indexed. In fact it is rather like those insurance policies that insure you against nearly everything that could happen to you in the way of illness until you come to read the small type, and then you find that practically everything that could possibly happen to you has been eliminated. And that's what we do with indexes. We are very proud of entering everything in the long and complicated indexes that we sometimes, though rarely, manage to persuade publishers to accept; but when we come down to it, all of us would have some rather unhappy moments if asked to list what we had not indexed. Another reading of the text might reveal many items that had not been indexed. Certain obvious ones we should be able to name: the foreword, the introduction, and the title page, and perhaps half the appendices and most of the illustrations. In fact, it is customary in Britain to confine the scope of the index to the body of the text, and usually readers accept the system without protests. But one must face the fact that in Britain people do not generally take indexes seriously at all. One proof of this is the case of a great government inquiry some years ago that filled the front pages of the evening papers and the back pages of the morning papers for days. It concerned a great scandal.[1] The resulting book ("paper" if you like) of evidence, findings, etc., was a foolscap volume which the newspapers noted included over one million words; and there was no index! So much for the British way of thinking about indexing. If one goes through new books today he will find a vast number with no indexes at all and most of the rest with bad ones. There are only a few good indexes, and so every

---

[1] *The Report of an Inquiry by a Tribunal* [the Lynskey Tribunal] *appointed to inquire into allegations reflecting on the official conduct of Ministers*, Cmd 7616 (1949)—Evidence, 34–322 [Editor].

year, when the Wheatley Medal for Indexing is to be awarded, it is a hard task to find one worthy of the award. The situation in the United States is different. There, most scholarly books are provided with indexes, and are expected to be so provided.

Here you have the anomaly of, on the one hand, the existence of a strong tendency for at least 2,000 years to compile indexes and, on the other hand, a far greater indifference to indexes on the part of all kinds of users of printed matter. How did this come about? It is a question of the needs of the expert users. Let us take, for example, the lawyers. When the early books of Statutes were issued they included what was called an index, although we would call it a detailed contents list. Printed at the front of the volume it was believed to be quite sufficient by the people who published these volumes of Statutes. Now, we know that what they thought and what the users thought were quite different, because in the back pages and on the blank pages of volumes that have survived from those days, the lawyers using these volumes in many cases wrote either complete or practically complete alphabetical lists of those Statutes in which they were principally interested. So here is one proof of the necessity of indexes and also some indication of how they were gradually being evolved. Another example may be cited. On the blank pages of old almanacs and Bibles it was the custom to enter notes at least of important things that people might want to refer to again. Now those who were compiling these amateur indexes had nothing really to guide them, although we do know, that as early as 900 A.D. people were already thinking in terms of alphabetical order. At least one encyclopedia at that time was arranged in this order. Here you have again a form of index, and certainly an early piece of evidence of the instinct to grasp what an index should be; but such efforts were regarded as freaks for about 300 years afterwards, and the main encyclopedias continued to be arranged in classified order. The same was true in the dictionaries. As late as the last part of the seventeenth century the first official French dictionary, the dictionary of the Académie Française, was published, not in alphabetical, but in classified order; and it was only with the second edition that the Académie yielded to the public demand and arranged the contents alphabetically.

Why there should have been this tremendous resistance to alphabetical order seems at first incomprehensible, but we do know that it was strong and that it continued to survive, in some cases even to grow. For example, as late as 1808 in a letter to Southey, Coleridge was scourging the idea of a decent encyclopedia being arranged by the accident of alphabetical order, and he did not appear at that time to have had any idea of the need of an index to the contents. But twenty years later he did; so here perhaps is part of the bridge to the modern concept of indexing.

Even when people did start having real indexes, it was in an extremely elementary form. In early Latin works, the compilers arranged their index entries by putting all items starting with the letter B together but in no special order, and so on. This was sufficient, they thought. Let us not laugh too heartily at their primitive methods of arranging indexes. We are not much better today. In some of our most learned volumes an index entry for page 631 may involve reading 500 or 600 words to find a reference which you are told appears on that page. How many of us have had the experience of trying to find in a hurry what this reference is supposed to be, and finding it only after the second reading or the third? So we too are primitive in much the same way. Over one thousand years ago it was thought sufficient to put all the A's together, and all the B's together, and so on, in no more detailed order, and today we say it is sufficient to give a reference that is within 500 or 600 words of what is wanted. How long would an atlas maker last in business if he failed to give a more exact reference to each place on the map? [2]

[2] Perhaps for large-page volumes with two columns, it might be feasible to indicate in which quarter of the page the given item is to be found as is done in *Encyclopaedia Britannica*.

Now, what in fact does good indexing do? In the first place it leads us quickly from the point of inquiry to the point of discovery. This is only one product of indexing. There are others too, some of them obvious and some rather surprising. Somebody once said that an index made a good book better and made no book wholly bad, or words to that effect; and every word of that saying is absolutely true. For example, the indexer, in indexing a book, is quickly aware whether it is a good book or a bad book. How is this so? As he reads the pages one by one he starts making his index entries, and what does he find? Starting off with high hopes, he thinks: Here is a subject into which the writer is really going to get his teeth. He makes one entry firmly and boldly and looks forward to adding several subsequent page numbers as he goes through the book, building up quite a body of information on this subject which clearly comes within the scope of the book. But then he finds that this first reference which he thought looked so promising is the only one that is any good at all, and that the subsequent references are superficial. The author has fought shy of this particular issue. This often happens in books that are called in publishers' catalogues "Comprehensive," "Challenging," "Vital," and all the rest of it. They are not. The indexer discovers all the nooks and crannies where the faults lie, and there are many of them in any book. Let us take one of the most obvious, one of the simplest, and, to the indexer, one of the most irritating of all. The author starts off by mentioning A, who in this case is Mr. Smith, and he spells him S-m-i-t-h on page 1. On page 224 he spells the name S-m-y-t-h, and on page 336, S-m-y-t-h-e, and so it goes on: the most common form of inconsistency. It does not happen so much in surnames as in Christian names. A man is John at one point and he is James in the next, and so on; and the author does not notice the inconsistency. There is a tremendous gap between the time when he was writing page 1 and when he was writing page 224; but the indexer notices the discrepancy immediately. Or let us hope he does, because otherwise both the publisher and the author will suffer. If the reviews are any good, both will be blamed. But since the indexer can prevent this, he should be brought in at an early stage.

But, while these are matters merely of spelling and poor memory—what we call "literals" for the most part—other more grievous errors appear. You sometimes find rather amusing examples of them in the *New Yorker*: little pieces at the ends of columns which are usually headed "Our Forgetful Authors" in which the latter on page 21 may give the heroine flaming red hair and on page 61 blue hair, and so on. The author has simply lost interest or has forgotten what he wrote earlier. Now, such books are usually not indexed at all, but one argument for indexing novels is simply to keep the novelist on the straight and narrow path. Perhaps this is not very important although you will find that Norman Knight is one, and the writer is another, who firmly thinks that any good novel should be indexed. The indexer discovers other things as well: inconsistency of statements, maybe inconsistency of dates, and so on. He also notices something else: inconsistency of coverage. Many authors find it very, very difficult not to stress their own particular "bee in the bonnet." This is quite natural, but from the point of view of the reader it is very irritating unless he has this same bee in *his* bonnet. A good index will show up this tendency. It will also do other things such as giving the reader of the book what he can never get otherwise—unless he has a photographic memory—namely a complete accumulation of information in that book on one particular person, or on one particular topic. It brings together all the scattered references so that, when an author disperses the information he has on a subject, or on a person, throughout a book, these can all be found together in one place in the index. This is very valuable, not only to the reader of the book, but also to those who use that book only to gather together references, with items from other books, facts, opinions, and so forth, on specific subjects and people—in other words, research workers. So there are several unexpected by-products of good indexing, but these are not always what the author or the publishers foresee. The good indexer can save a publisher quite a lot of money. In a recent case concerning a periodical, a lot of money, red tape, and embarrassment could have been saved had indexing been done. There was a reference to a rather scandalous case that happened a few years ago, a reference which the indexer would automatically have picked up and recognized from the content to be incorrect. He would have been able to save the publisher some embarrassment by notifying the latter in advance of publication. As it was, every issue of that journal had to be withdrawn and replaced.

The indexer is the one person who really scrutinizes the pages from all points of view. The printer looks out for questions of spelling, punctuation, layout, typography, and so on. The publisher is on the lookout for different errors. He knows he can rely upon his printer for most things, although the good publisher will always urge his printer to suggest improvements. But the publisher is on guard against the possibility of serious error, and is also watching for com-mercial possibilities—in some cases the film and broadcast-ing rights, and so on. So these people are looking at the book from different points of view. But the indexer goes through the text line by line trying to analyze the material into some kind of coherent scheme. Almost mechanically the faults begin to show up. The misspellings, the misstate-ments of fact, the ambiguities, the overlapping, the poor construction—everything of this kind becomes embarrass-ingly apparent to the indexer. Unfortunately, usually far too late, he is apt to be called in at the last moment.

To return for a moment to the arrangement of indexes. The very early people thought it sufficient to group items simply under the initial letter of the alphabet. This went on for a long time. They were still doing it, in some places, in the seventeenth century. But with the eighteenth century a new idea really arrived: close alphabetical indexing. It is to be found in Diderot's *Encyclopédie*, which is alphabetically arranged. But even with a good grasp of alphabetical indexing, they were extraordinarily stubborn about developing these ideas. Take, for example, the cumulative indexes to the early volumes of the *Gentleman's Magazine* and the *Annual Register*. It quickly became clear that there was a market for cumulative indexes to these magnificent books of reference. So there came into existence indexes of persons mentioned in the individual volumes. For the most part these indexes were quite good. The surnames were arranged, with occasional exceptions, in strict alphabetical order; but then came the rub. All the Joneses were put together without any differentiation between them, without any indication of their different initials. This system applied not only to the Joneses, but to the Smiths and Robinsons and Browns and all the rest. Nobody has ever sat down to revising these indexes, which is a great pity because people are continuing to waste time in using them. Here again was this almost blind attitude to proper alphabetical indexes, and this in spite of the fact that Dr. Johnson had created a magnificent dictionary, a very complicated one, in a model alphabetical order.

Not only was there this resistance to learning how to arrange indexes and what to put in them; there was still a great resistance to having indexes at all. Take the *Britannica*. When that first came out, just two hundred years ago, there was no index because people thought that its arrangement in alphabetical order made one unnecessary. It was not until the 6th or 7th edition, some sixty or seventy years later, right up into the middle of the nineteenth century, that the *Britannica* first gave in and provided an index, and this only because a competitive encyclopedia was actually compiling one at that time. Right up to 1840 they were still resisting this idea, whereas nowadays, when you buy any encyclopedia (whether the *Britannica* or *Chambers's* or any other), one of the very first things you look at—or if you don't the salesman points it out—is the index. An index does reveal inconsistencies and, therefore, the encyclopedia makers keep a permanent indexing staff to watch closely for such items. Otherwise any encyclopedia, because it contains millions and millions of words, could include thousands of inconsistencies, and direct or indirect contradictions. So, here is another very, very useful by-product of indexing.

There are all kinds of reasons for having an index in addition to the purely obvious one of leading the reader from one place to another. But if there are going to be indexes, then they must be inclusive. Nothing is more irritating than to have to reread a book in order to find something one remembers having read in it previously. Thus, if an index is to be really comprehensive it will inevitably be larger than the average index today. One has only to look at some of the larger law books to see how great a place the index is beginning to take in any serious work. Other books too have very lengthy indexes. In fact, with encyclopedias the index now constitutes between one-tenth and one-twentieth of the total mass of material. That is a rather interesting indication of the future of indexes. Since an index to an encyclopedia is printed in smaller type than the text with perhaps four columns to a page, it is really very much larger than this proportion. But if it is between one-tenth and one-twentieth and is still inadequate, what should its size be? The writer sometimes opens a book, looks at the number of pages, and compares it with the number of pages for the index. Too often the size of the index is an accident. It may be the right length, it may not. But, if one has a look at every book that he handles and compares the size of the index, he will come up with some very interesting findings. First of all one will rarely find a book that devotes more than one-twentieth of the text space to the index: that is, for a book of two hundred pages one will seldom find an index of ten pages—in Britain that would be regarded as excessive, and in the United States not quite so excessive. But it is far more likely that one will find that the book has an index only one-thirtieth or one-fortieth of the textual space. That cannot be a very detailed index. In the average index one will find references, perhaps, to five or six items on one page. That is very few, especially when one realizes that, because the indexer feels he must index every name, too little room is left for the ideas. You may get quite an elaborate index which will mention almost every name in the book (apart from those in the credits, foreword, illustrations, appendices) but the subject matter will often have been very badly done. What are the reasons for this? First, the indexer may have missed it. Second, and more likely, his index entry is under another heading which he thinks is the right one. Third, he may have misunderstood it and entered it under some other category entirely. Here another important factor comes into play: the rapport which is essential between the author, the indexer, and the readers. And by readers is meant the readers of today, of twenty years hence, and of fifty years hence. What the author intended can easily be misinterpreted by the indexer for several reasons. Even if the indexer knows something about the subject, this may not be sufficient. A good author should be in advance of his public; in other words, he should know something the public does not know. This demands close collaboration between the indexer and the author, because otherwise the new concepts are liable to be only partially noted in the index. And another important factor is that if it is an important book, a valuable book, a book of lasting interest to people, the index is being compiled not for today only but for the readers twenty and fifty years hence. We must at least make an effort to think ahead about the people in those future days, if the index is to be of use as a research or reference tool.

There is another factor that has not been mentioned, a very important one. It is a very common and very dangerous one, little known to the public, and vitally affecting the work. This is the practice of modern publishers by which the indexer rarely gets the text to work on until the page proofs are issued. He may get a glimpse of the book in manuscript or in galley-proof form, but he cannot do very much about it until the page proofs arrive. Then he must get a move on. But, while he is getting a move on with his indexing, the publishers, printers, and the author are all pushing their own work; the author may be altering his text, the publisher may be urging him to alter other things in his text, and the printers may be picking up small points—and printers are very good at picking up such things—which must be altered. Is the indexer always warned of these alterations? Unfortunately, no. Especially he rarely sees any added material or the illustrations that are to go into the book. These are very often kept separate from the page proofs and may even be prepared by a different wing of the printers, perhaps—in the case of color printing—by some other printer altogether. Thus for various reasons there are odd bits of the book that the indexer may well miss. Now this is a bad situation, because it results in an imperfect index; and to rectify it the public, which is in fact paying for the index, must make a fuss. If an index constitutes one-twentieth of a book, then probably one-twentieth of the price of the book is for that index; it is not free of charge. And while one hopes that the book itself will be free of textual errors and misdirection, he also should be able to expect a perfect index or one as near perfect as possible. How much effective pressure the public can bring to bear on publishers is very doubtful indeed in most cases; but in one field, at any rate, the presence of a good index surely helps to sell the book. Let us take, for example, *Whitaker's Almanack*. The writer is quite convinced in his own mind that one of the reasons for its tremendous success over the years has been that, unlike many of its nineteenth-century rivals, the index has been quite outstanding. It may not be perfect, but it is a very, very good index, a very sensible one, and one that has stood the test of time. The presence or absence of such an index is one of the reasons why some reference publications succeed and some do not.

Let us turn to one more point on indexing: if our book indexes are bad, and many are, those to journals, when they exist, are worse. They are appalling. There are a thousand different reasons why no faith can be put in most periodical indexes, although occasionally there is a good one. *The Indexer*, for example, has to have a good one in order to survive. One of the ways of bringing pressure to bear on publishers is to point out that our subscription to a journal should include a good strong index.

But now what constitutes a good strong index in a journal? Those who use libraries must have noticed with some surprise how different libraries handle the binding of their periodicals. Some bind the whole journals, covers and all, and place the index in front or at the back, as they prefer. Others rip the covers off but leave the rest. Others rip all the advertisements off as well as the covers, put all the text together in front, and all the covers and all the advertisements together at the back. Still others tear off and throw away all the covers and all the advertisements (and sometimes, without knowing it, part of the text as well) and bind up the remainder. Now, apart from the inconsistency of these practices, what are we doing? It seems to the writer in the first case that most libraries are making certain that there is no complete set anywhere. We know in the case of the indexes to most journals—where they exist—that they certainly do not cover the advertisements, although these are sometimes important, including as they do pictures of machinery, tools, and people, and, very often, prices, addresses, and other details. Sometimes the user needs that information more than the very learned research articles in the middle of the journal. There is a good case to be made, if not for a comprehensive index printed in the journals, at least for a manuscript one. The writer believes that all indexes should be printed on one side of the page only, and on good paper, so that one can write on the blank page the points he would like to see indexed. Such a practice would help a great deal, because each one of us has a very individual approach to an index. There is one more very serious aspect of indexing to think about, and that is: How much of an index is the indexer's dream, and how much is what anybody uses? How often in reading index entries does the reader ask: Who on earth would have thought of looking under that heading? Why did the indexer choose it? Surely headings which appear useless could be due to rule-of-thumb indexing which always involves the danger of inflating the index without any corresponding gain in its value.

Now, to get down to essentials. If an index of only three entries can bring the reader quickly to any point in a book that he wants, then it is probably a good index, and one of forty pages with 1,200 entries will be no better. Thus, size in indexes, although important, is not a prerequisite. The really important thing is quality. Since an index of three entries could never deliver us to all the places we want to go, because what might suit one, would never suit all, it is obviously going to be much longer than that. But the writer is convinced, and many indexers feel the same way, that nearly every index is full of a lot of dead wood. But how is it to be cut out? By a more careful study of this problem. If only there was an index in a generally used book which would react every time somebody used an actual index entry! Those index entries which were well used would light up each time and those which were never used would remain dark. Since there is no such system yet, some other way must be found to make indexes more concise. The hard truth is that it is very difficult to get more space for an index, and before indexers try to get more they had better make certain that they are making the utmost use, the best use, of what they already have.

# THE ELEMENTS OF BOOK INDEXING, PART II

ROBERT L. COLLISON

It is impossible to know in theory how good an indexer one is and whether one really wants to do indexing. It is an occupation that attracts all kinds of people, rather as teaching does, until it is actually tried; then either it is the job of a lifetime or the last thing on earth they want to go on doing. No one knows until he actually comes to do it what the result will be. This does no harm because, even if one learns that he does not want to index, one has accomplished something else of value. He has become better informed about indexes and indexing; he probably knows better how to use an index; and he will probably be a little more outspoken about bad indexes or the lack of indexes. Even a good index can be improved. For example, an index that the writer uses quite frequently is the magnificent one in the Statistical Abstract of the United States. This annual volume has a fascinating index at the end, done with great care, but it could be improved. For example, one table shows the livestock in each of the states, so that the user can work out quite easily the number of milch cows, the number of hogs, the number of sheep, the number of all cattle, and so forth, in each state. The table is headed quite clearly "Livestock on Farms–Number, by States." But under "Livestock" in the index there is no direct reference to this table. Instead there is one to: "*See* Animals, domestic, and also Individual

Classes." It would be just as easy to give a direct reference under "Livestock," and so save the user's time. This shows the gulf between the indexer and the user. The former is working on definite theoretical lines; but had he been a user and had looked up "Livestock" about sixteen times before remembering that references would be under "Animals, domestic," he would have given direct references under "Livestock." So, the more one knows about indexing, whether or not he decides to become an indexer, the better for everyone.

The only way of discovering whether one is an indexer or not is to index a book. With indexing one starts off so happily and with great and high hopes—he is going to make a *good* index. How does he go about it? One basic thing to be accepted straight away is that each subject, each name, each title, each idea, must be entered on a separate slip or card, so that they can be arranged in many different patterns. Now this seems obvious, and yet nearly everybody breaks the rule. They break it and regret it, and yet they break it again and again. (In the case of a *very* small work, it may be possible to compile the whole of an index in a little thumb-index notebook. But that is for very small works, such as an index to the staff regulations of a small organization. It will not work for any index above some 500 references.)

There are many, many different ways of going about practical indexing, and since indexing is still in the experimental stage, any way that a given indexer finds effective is the right one for him, and he does not have to worry about how someone else indexes. On the other hand, in planning in advance it is well to be aware of how others index in order to have as complete a choice as possible of the various methods. In any case, one must have a flexible index, something that can be arranged and rearranged. An important thing is to keep in mind the conditions in which indexing is carried out.

The index entries are on separate sheets, cards, or slips, and they can come apart or get into the wrong order.

Again, one is probably not entirely concentrating on one page at a time, but may be turning back to other pages to compare notes. It is therefore advisable not to index on the deck of a ship, for example, or on the windy edge of cliffs; what is needed is a quiet, warm, well-lit place with no drafts, and some fair amount of peace.

In considering what materials to use, one must not be tempted into using inefficient or insubstantial tools. Take the slips or cards that are going to be used. The essential thing is that they should all be of the same size, otherwise they are very difficult to sort and resort. The need is for something which is precise in its measurements and which has very clean edges that are very elastic and springy so that they can be flicked through the fingers, and will stand up to any amount of hard wear. They must have a good surface not only for writing on, but also for erasing, rewriting, overwriting, and so on. Ready-made index cards or slips are available in most stationery shops. Or a friendly printer will make thousands of indexing slips rather more cheaply out of odds and ends of paper. A card is more expensive, at least in Britain, but can be used two or three times, because it stands up to quite a lot of hard wear. Moreover, it is much easier to handle and so is a time saver. One needs to decide whether the initial cheapness of one type of material is not more than counterbalanced by the savings from the expensive but a more lasting form. If cards are used, they should be very thin, tough, and springy; if slips, something substantial with a fairly shiny type of calendered surface.

What size should these cards or slips be? The right size is the one that best suits the indexer. A sheet of $8 \times 10$ writing paper can be folded to give four slips, each $8'' \times 2\frac{1}{2}''$, and many people find this a very acceptable form of indexing slip. Most professional librarians who are engaged in this kind of work will choose quite a different shape altogether. They are used to the standard catalogue card, approximately $5'' \times 3''$, and so instinctively use a $5'' \times 3''$ slip when indexing. As has been stated, these are readily available from stationers. Other people prefer a slightly larger slip, 6″ × 3″ or 6″ × 4″. These sizes are in general use although one will find many variations. The size of the card or slip does not matter greatly, but it is worth experimenting to find out which one best suits the indexer, because he is going to have to live with the cards or slips.

What kind of container should one use for the index entries? Basically it is some kind of box, in which the cards or slips can be moved up and down quite easily, with their tops slightly projecting so that they can be handled at the side as well as from the top. Some people use an old shoe box, cutting down the sides slightly to show the upper half-inch or inch of the slips. Others who use 5″ × 3″ cards can get an old wooden or fiber catalogue drawer to house them, or even the cardboard box in which the blank cards came. As one gets more and more professional at this, he will probably conclude that properly made, even if initially expensive, equipment is the best. To be sure, many people continue to go on in quite a makeshift fashion and do extraordinarily well. But the one thing on which costs should not be cut is quality of the material: good quality will save a lot of hard work.

When writing on cards or slips one needs to be wary of the effect of friction. Since the cards are constantly being moved backwards and forwards there is tremendous friction which induces smudging, especially if one is using a soft pencil. There will be a tendency for the outlines of figures representing the page references to get smudged or blurred. A runny ink will have much the same effect. Experiments will help one to find a ball-point pen or a good pencil, which does not smudge or blur. Nothing is more irritating in indexing than to have written a figure and then to find that it has been blurred out of all recognition.[1] It means that one must check the entry again.

These may seem very elementary counsels, but they can save a lot of trouble. Once an indexer has a system set up

[1] The *sfumato* effect pleases painters but not printers!

to his own satisfaction, he can begin the actual work of indexing.

Here the writer suggests that it is absolutely essential, if the publisher gives you time, to read the book through just before indexing it. This again is so obvious a point that it is a shame it should have to be said, but the publisher usually puts such pressure of time on the indexer that the latter is tempted to plunge straight into his indexing. If he does, without first reading the text, he is bound to feel uncertain of himself and is likely to produce an unbalanced index. But, if he reads through the book he will get the feel of it. When the writer is indexing a book, he likes to read it twice; then he gets a very good idea of the balance of subjects, of what things he should emphasize, and so on. Otherwise one may perhaps index all the names on the first two pages as well as a great many subjects in great detail, and then suddenly start cutting down. In the end he has to do the whole thing over again because he did not properly weigh the whole picture.

Having already read the book and obtained some idea of the feel of it, one can start making index entries. Each card or slip should be reserved for a single subject, a single name, a single idea, and so forth, but not necessarily for a single reference. The question of whether or not the card should be kept for a single reference or for many references, is debatable, and indexers will debate it until the end of time. Whether every time the subject of, say, "Fisheries" comes up one should make a new card or slip, or instead enter the additional page reference on the original slip. However, there is no excuse at all for putting different subjects on the same card merely because they are close at hand, such as "Fisheries" and "Flags." That bad practice will land one in trouble in most cases. But to return to the practice of putting all the references to "Fisheries" on one card. This seems economical, sensible, and sane. But, what is involved here? Let us say that the initial reference to "Fisheries" is on page 31, and the next on page 264. How does one discover the card with the initial entry? Since he may have quite forgotten the first entry by the time he reaches the second on page 264, is not the only thing to do the keeping of the cards in alphabetical order? Then one is able to check any entry made before. What is the routine for this? When *does* the indexer put his cards in alphabetical order? At the very time that he makes an entry on one? Or at the end of a page? Or at the end of a chapter? In using any one of these methods, the indexer must work out a system which will enable him to keep track of his place even when faced with interruptions. All this means that the choice of materials and of method of working must be considered very, very carefully. The writer has always referred to indexing as a cottage industry—and long may it go on!— but if it is a cottage industry it must be capable of coping with the kettle boiling over and the children coming home from school; otherwise it is going to produce very bad indexes.

The question as to whether one should or should not arrange the cards straight away in alphabetical order has far more significance than the narrow one of being able to enter further references on cards already made. If it were only that, it would not be worth considering, because there is a decided advantage in keeping the cards in page number order until the initial indexing is completed. For one thing, in the case of interruptions the top card will represent the exact point reached when the interruption occurred. Second, if one decides, as he will inevitably when first indexing, that he has done a very bad job on the initial pages, he can then restore the balance with a sure hand: he knows exactly what he has indexed on any particular page, and so forth. But this is impossible if all the cards have already been filed in alphabetical order.

There is another method not mentioned so far. There are a number of indexers who do not write cards at all; they type them, using continuous stationery perforated horizontally. At the end of the book these slips or cards are separated and sorted. But here, too, there are disadvantages, because if all slips are kept in the order of the pages— either on cards or by the perforated stationery method on the typewriter—then a separate slip will have to be made for every fresh mention of a subject, no matter how often this is repeated. One may, in fact, type the same name a hundred or two hundred or five hundred times. This may seem a terrible waste of time. But what about the time wasted in searching for the original card in the alphabetical files?

All these points must be considered, for they condition the choice of materials and the method of working. If a separate slip is made for every subject, no matter how many times it is mentioned, afterwards there is a tremendous amount of editorial work to be done. All references to a single subject must be assembled on one card or slip. On the other hand, if they are already assembled on one slip there is another kind of trouble. With any complicated subject they must be sorted out according to their various subcategories, and one might find such sorting simpler to do if each reference was on a separate slip.

The main thing in considering the choice of method is not to be especially worried about it, but to keep all the possibilities in mind. (An advantage of the continuous stationery method over cards is that it can be allied to another system where the underpart of these continuous stationery slips is gummed so that they can be stuck into place on a backing sheet ready for the printer.)

The printer must have a clear script of some kind from which he is able to set type. Most printers accept cards or slips. A few insist that the index be in typescript form on sheets of paper. Some of them will even accept handwritten slips; and in fact many newspaper indexes, where they are printed, are certainly built up from such slips. But this depends on truly legible writing. There is much to be said for a good handwritten slip: it can bring out nuances that cannot be conveyed by typescript. For example, on a hand-written slip one can show varying sizes of type. If the indexer wishes to put a very small subscript number to indicate a note number, a footnote number, and so on, he can do it in handwriting, but not easily on the typewriter.

34

Another important point in practical indexing is to keep the number of cards or slips under control, and this affects one's choice of methods. For example, it is quite easy to handle about a thousand cards. That number will go into a box of not more than a foot in length, and one advantage of a container of that size is that it can be handled quite easily. Here is another argument on the side of keeping the slips in alphabetical order. A thousand cards may represent anything up to three or four thousand references, perhaps more in the case of a tightly knit book on a limited subject.

On the card or slip itself, the writer suggests that the heading should not be written in capitals throughout the word but only with initial caps. Page numbers should be clearly set apart from the words in the entry, particularly where that includes figures—such as in historical entries incorporating dates. And the page numbers themselves should always be kept in numerical order: this makes checking easier. It is essential, after one has written a page reference on a slip, to check the page number at once. Never break this rule. Sometimes the mind plays tricks, and when one has finished page 19, he does not always react automatically to writing page 20 for all the entries on the following page. Particularly if one is getting tired, he will still write page 19 for the first two or three references on page 20. So check back immediately for accuracy of reference.

As the indexer goes on making entries for subjects, he will begin to get various ideas about the form of the index and about developments of the index, ideas which he intends to carry out in the editorial stage. To keep track of these it is well to have a section in front of one's sequence, headed "Notes," and to put each idea on a separate card or slip, filing it under "Notes." Otherwise these ideas may be forgotten. Some indexers prefer to make such notes in a notebook. The important thing is to see that they are registered as one thinks about them.

Mistakes that the author or the printer has made should be called to the attention of the publishers as quickly as possible. That is part of the indexer's function, for it helps to ensure that the book will be as nearly perfect as possible.

If one could index a whole book in a single evening at a single session, there would be fewer problems. One could simply sit down, enter into the whole spirit of the thing, and emerge with a well-knit product—it would have been a thoroughly enjoyable operation. But no book can be indexed in so short a period. And since the index making will be spread over a fairly long period, the indexer's mind is going to change as he works through the book, and he will not always maintain exactly the same attitude to the text. This means that he may use different headings on different days without realizing it. If he recognizes this problem in advance, he can make provision for the synonyms, alternate headings, spellings, and so on, which must be kept in mind. To establish consistency he must be firm with himself at the start: as a rule people when indexing, especially when they are new to it, want to get a move on. But most indexers learn that sooner or later they come up against the problem, that they cannot hurry, that they have to work at a steady pace, and that there are no really good short cuts. Some people index almost automatically, but they are very rare indeed: and they usually have exceptional memories which act as secondary indexes.

When the cards or slips begin to build up, it is wise to spend even five minutes looking through the ones already made, just to see how the index is shaping. Just a glance will repay the effort. To test this point in advance, take the index to some well-known book, and instead of reading the book start reading the index. This is a terrible test for any book. As you go through the index you may notice inconsistencies, simply because the indexer did not examine his work as a whole. A short index to a book may show a lack of balance, a lack of consistency, and sometimes other horrors. Such a test will show that usually one is making exactly the same mistakes oneself.

There are all kinds of tasks which the beginner can carry out with indexes to test his own ability and his own real interest in it. For example, he can take quite a small work, something perhaps only twenty pages long, which has an index. Without looking at the index, let him index the whole text himself, from start to finish, the way he thinks it ought to be done. Then when he has finished his index, let him compare it with the index already in the book or pamphlet. In one respect his index will probably be better than the printed one, because he wanted to see how well he could do the job. On the other hand, the compiler of the printed index probably knew the subject better and therefore he will have given due emphasis to important aspects that the beginner would not have thought of. Thus the latter will actually have learned something new about indexing. Any sort of test is rewarding and is a valuable way of self-training for this type of work. The best teachers in the world are the works of indexers who have gone before and done it very well.

The indexer must have at hand certain reference tools. First, a dictionary to check spellings, especially of controversial words. Most British indexers would choose *Chambers's Mid-20th Century Dictionary* or the *Concise Oxford Dictionary*. American indexers usually consult *Webster's New International Dictionary*. In any case, the indexer must choose one dictionary and stick to it for spelling and also, what is far more important, for definition of words. Second, since the form of a town's name, a country's name, and so on, is terribly important, a guide is needed here, perhaps in fact two guides: a good up-to-date atlas and a good gazetteer. These will also clear up questions of whether a place is in one country or another, and so forth. Third, to check people's names, the indexers should have a small biographical dictionary, possibly *Chambers's Biographical Dictionary* or *Webster's Biographical Dictionary*. Many other reference books[2] would also be useful, but these three groups are

[2] Notably a good index to a book on the same subject as that on which the indexer is working, to be used as a model; or else a standard list of subject headings such as the one issued by the Library of Congress. Other useful tools include authority lists, thesauruses, inverted cross-reference files, and other devices used for vocabulary control in indexing. [Editor]

absolutely essential: a dictionary, a biographical dictionary, and an atlas-cum-gazetteer of some kind. With these aids the indexer *must* check everything. For example, authors very often refer to a person by his surname only. This is no good in an index, where his complete name or identification must be given, if possible. For this the indexer may have to consult other than the reference books suggested above, and so must allow sufficient time, either to get to a library or to write to a library or somebody else about the matter. This must be done from the start; one must be able to get these things checked and thoroughly checked. Waiting until the actual process of indexing is finished is too late. The best way would be to make notes in the preliminary reading of the book, so that things that must be looked up elsewhere can be checked while the process of indexing is going on. The indexer can either do the work himself or ask somebody else to do it; then the index will not be held up on the one hand, nor on the other hand have inadequate entries.

There is more to indexing than the clerical process of making entries for names and places and the more obvious subjects. But can it be mechanized? Well, we are getting very close to this. Already concordances, which are the most elementary form of index, are being compiled by computers; a recent example is that for Walt Whitman's *Leaves of Grass* which was done entirely by computer. The possibilities here are immense. Many voluminous authors are waiting for this to be done: Bernard Shaw, Winston Churchill, and so on. Here are clear subjects for the use of a computer. But the translation of words into ideas is what distinguishes the index from the concordance. The index is a further refinement. Nevertheless the computer can save a lot of time. It can be instructed to index every word in the book except such things as definite and indefinite articles. This will remove the drudgery from the task and, while not making the job shorter, can make it more thorough and help the indexer to sidestep some of the more tiring routine work that has to be done now.

Whether or not you are an indexer by nature can be tested by the following:

## Practical Exercise

Compile your own fairly comprehensive index to the first two chapters ("The Elements of Book Indexing," Parts I and II). Then compare your result with the corresponding entries (page references 14–38) in the index at the end of this book. The index entries concerned will be easily recognized as their page references alone are printed in italics.

## 3

# ALPHABETICAL ARRANGEMENT

G. NORMAN KNIGHT

## Introduction

It is not absolutely essential for an index to be arranged alphabetically. For instance, in a list of tools in use in a given factory, it may be more convenient to have them arranged, not by a description of each tool, but numerically according to the tools' factory numbers. And, as we shall see, it is possible, even in an alphabetical index, to have some parts arranged nonalphabetically.

But for most practical purposes, and notably in the case of the indexes for books and periodicals, alphabetical arrangement is so much more convenient than any other system that it has become almost universal.

## Transliteration

According to the *British Standard of Alphabetical Arrangement* (*B.S. 1749:1951*),[1] which costs two shillings and sixpence and is very brief but quite useful, the basis of arrangement should be the order of the English alphabet. This applies only to books and journals written in English, since the International Organization for Standardization (I.S.O.)

[1] As this volume goes to press, the Standard is being revised by a subcommittee of the British Standards Institution. Such material changes as have already been agreed (June 1967) are incorporated or referred to in this chapter.

left the standardizing bodies of individual countries to establish their own national standards in this matter.

When words written in a non-Roman alphabet are to be used as key words in an index, they must be arranged as if transliterated in accordance with recognized schemes. Should any indexer be so unlucky as to come across any such indexable non-Roman-alphabet words in the text of a book for which he is preparing the index, I can only recommend that he consult the standard work on transliterating the given language, such as:

| | |
|---|---|
| Cyrillic and modern Greek | B.S. 2979:1958 |
| Arabic | I.S.O./R 233; B.S. 4280:1958 |
| Hebrew | I.S.O./R 259 |
| Chinese | the Wade-Giles system |

The last item is contained in the 2-volume *Chinese-English Dictionary* by H. A. Giles (London, 1912). Another extensive bibliography on the indexing and transcription of Chinese characters is to be found in a useful article by H. D. Talbot in *The Indexer*, Vol. II, No. 3 (1961), pp. 102–103.

Cyrillic includes Russian. It so happens that the introduction of a new Russian orthography was one of the earliest acts of the Soviet government after the Revolution of 1917, and books now printed in the U.S.S.R. must conform to the new spelling. Under this the old letter "yat" (or "ie") becomes "e," so that Soviet is now spelled Sovet. But I would not advise the use of the latter form in indexes, unless it is so spelled in the text.

## Accents, Diacritical Marks, and Apostrophes

According to both the *British Standard of Alphabetical Arrangement*, already referred to, and the British Standard *The Preparation of Indexes* (B.S. 3700:1964) the first two of these items do not affect the alphabetical order. Thus we might find the following examples (from Collison's *Indexing Books*, 1962):

Alès
Ålesund

Älvsborg
Anécho
Anegada Is.
Aswân
Asyût
Bachău

Both the German umlaut ö and the Danish ø are treated as o and not as oe. Thus Marshal von Göring, if spelled that way in the text, is to be listed in the index (appropriately enough, some may say) after "Gorilla." But there should be a cross reference from "Goering," where the index user is likely to look.

This is the British Standards rule and British indexers must abide by it. Nevertheless the complete disregarding of modified letters can be dangerous in any index used internationally.

Thus, Germans who have no typewriter containing ä, ö, ü, write these letters as ae, oe, ue, and this practice would affect the alphabetical indexing order, e.g., of words like Öl (Oel). As a rule Americans follow this method. Again, Scandinavians put words beginning with AE and Ø after Z in the alphabet, while the Danes put Å (Aa) after that letter. Then there is the Polish Ł, which is a different letter from L. Cross references provide the only good answer to the problem.

Apostrophes are not dealt with in the British Standard of Indexing. My own practice has always been to place a word in the possessive case immediately after the last example of the word without an apostrophe. Thus:

Cox, Percival
Cox, Terence
Cox's Orange Pippins
Coxe, Henry

But Collison (in his *Indexing Books*) suggests that *Chambers's Encyclopaedia* should follow Chamberson. The indexer himself must follow whichever method he thinks the better.[2]

---

[2]But it is understood that the new Alphabetical Arrangement Standard (see footnote, p. 40) will recommend (in the interests of computer-compiled indexes) that *all* apostrophes be "treated as spaces."

Perhaps it should be added that my method is the one used in the English telephone directories, which on the whole can be regarded as models of good indexing. Thus:

Graham, Z.
Graham's Stores
Graham-Brown, T. J.

This system has the advantage of juxtaposing all holders of the same name, whereas under the Collison system there might be a considerable interval of extraneous names between some possessive and other examples of the same name.

On the other hand, an apostrophe denoting an elision and not the possessive case should be ignored as affecting the order. Thus, the song "It's a Long Way to Tipperary" or the book *It's Never Too Late to Mend* would come between Itinerary and Iturea.

## Numerals

Instances of these in the text which may be required as part of indexing headings can also be bothersome. The British Standard of Indexing rule is quite plain: numerals shall be arranged as if spelled out (in the corresponding language).

0 spell out as nought[3]
3 arranged as three
5% arranged as five per cent
31  arranged as thirty-one
328 arranged as three hundred and twenty-eight
1345 (if a date) thirteen forty-five
        (otherwise) one thousand three hundred and forty-five
100, 1000, etc. one hundred, one thousand, NOT a hundred, etc.

But in the case of such a title as *100 Best Stories*, I would feel disposed to index it under Hu for Hundred. Like all the rules of indexing, this one must be tempered with a good deal of common sense.

Recently I have been engaged on indexing the first volume of Randolph Churchill's official life of his father.

[3]In international practice, *zero* is preferred.

Now almost the whole of Sir Winston's military career was spent in the 4th Hussars, which accordingly required a sizable entry in the index. In the text it is invariably referred to numerically as the 4th Hussars. But in my index I spelled it boldly, Fourth Hussars, the, — with a cross reference from Hussars, 4th.

In order to assist the programmers of computer-produced indexes, the revisers of the British Standard (see footnote on page 40) recommend that, whenever possible, numerals should not merely be arranged as if spelled out, but should be actually spelled out. As the majority of indexers, however, still work manually, the writer ventures to suggest that this recommendation need not necessarily affect them.

As regards foreign titles or texts:

*20 ans après* as *Vingt ans après*
*1001 Nacht* as *Tausend und eine Nacht*
*1001 Nights* as *Thousand and One Nights, A*

There is, however, one important exception: where the numeral marks one of a series, it would be madness to use alphabetical order. And so the items would be listed serially, as follows:

| | | |
|---|---|---|
| Henry IV, King of England | Uranium 235 | 1, 2, 3-xylenol |
| Henry VIII, King of England | Uranium 236 | 1, 2, 5-xylenol |
| Henry IV, King of France | Uranium 238 | 1, 3, 4-xylenol |

This reminds the writer that recently an American computer, whose assistance had been invoked in compiling an important historico-religious work, "dug in its heels" against such a numerical order, insisting upon a strictly alphabetical sequence. Consequently, unless the machine can be "brought to heel" (to vary the metaphor), one may expect to see certain occupants of the Holy See egregiously listed as follows:

| | | | |
|---|---|---|---|
| Pius VIII | Pius I [First] | Pius II | Pius X |
| Pius XI | Pius IV | Pius VII | Pius III |
| Pius V | Pius IX | Pius VI | Pius XII |

So also one would use a numerical order in subheadings, even when the words are actually spelled out:

Society of Indexers, The:
First Annual Report
Second Annual Report
Fourth Annual Report
*Journal* of,

But *not* where the numbers do not indicate a series:

100 Years War (under H)
7 Years War (under S)
30 Years War (under T)

## Other Nonalphabetical Orders

*Subheadings.* Particularly in subheadings it is sometimes better to desert alphabetical order in favor of a chronological or evolutionary or other systematic order, as for instance:

Geological eras:
Paleozoic
Mesozoic
Tertiary
Quaternary
Pleistocene
Glacial (Ice Age)
Land routes:
Motorways: M 1 . . .; M 2 . . .
Major A roads: A 1 . . . etc.
Minor B roads: B . . .
Lanes or tracks . . .

European history:
12th century
13th century
14th century

The British Standard of Indexing has a whole section on "Systematic (nonalphabetical) indexes," in which it is stated that "although alphabetical arrangement is by far the commonest method used in publications (as distinct from library catalogues and card information files), yet classified, numerical, or chronological order of main headings and subheadings may sometimes be of value—for instance, in a treatise on chemistry or mineralogy, or in a book on expeditions and voyages, or in a history of a particular country or period, e.g.

> 1960: Spring . . .; Summer . . .; Autumn . . .; Winter . . .
> 1962: January . . .; February . . . ; May . . . ; September . . .
> etc."

The chronological order is sometimes useful in the case of "run-on" subheadings in the index to a history or biography, where it will probably correspond with the page sequence in the text.

*Symbols.* As with numbers, so as a rule symbols should be arranged in an index as if they were spelled out. (The revisers of the *British Standard of Alphabetical Arrangement* recommend that they shall actually be spelled out.)

> − as if minus
> + as if plus
> = as if equals
> % as if per cent

It is difficult to imagine any instance where these symbols would come as the key word of an entry, but they might well come as the second word and so affect the order of other entries with the same key word.

*Ampersand.* Similarly the ampersand (&) should usually be spelled out as "and"; in the unlikely event of its occuring as a key word it must be spelled out as "ampersand." It should be noted, however, that in the British and American telephone directories it is ignored. There the alphabetical order is determined by the following word. Thus:

> Bourne Bros.
> Bourne & Co. Ltd.
> Bourne, Higgs & Co.
> Bourne & Hollingsworth

It is up to the indexer to decide which order to adopt. But it is worth noticing that the British Standard seems to support the telephone directory usage by expressly allowing "connecting articles, conjunctions [such as the ampersand] in proper names or titles beginning with the same word (organizations, periodicals, etc.) to be ignored in alphabetization in order to obtain a single A/Z array of subsequent significant words." It adds that they should be parenthesized or subordinated typographically and gives the following examples:

| | |
|---|---|
| Bulletin (d') Hygiène | Society (of) Indexers |
| Bulletin (de l') Institut Pasteur | Society (for the) Promotion of |
| Bulletin metéorologique | Christian Knowledge |
| Bulletin (du) Photoclub de Nice | Society (of) Radiographers |
| | Society (for) Visiting Scientists |

But this is a subject that really concerns Compound Headings, dealt with later.

## Simple Abbreviations

By "simple" is meant one-word abbreviations, as opposed to compound abbreviations, which will be discussed later.

Single letter abbreviations are naturally placed at the beginning of that letter, others following in strict alphabetical order as spelled:

P, *see* Phosphorus
Parabolas
Pb, *see* Lead

Other abbreviations are also alphabetized as spelled in the contracted form with the exceptions of Mc and M' and also St.

*Mac, Mc, and M'.* All three are indexed as if they were simply "Mac" (which in effect they are), the order being determined by the succeeding letter:

Mac goes to school
Macadam (*see also* Tarmac)
McAdam, E. D.
Macbeth
McCrystol, R. G.
Machinery
M'Kenzie, Alistair
Mackenzie, Compton
Macmillan, Rt. Hon. Harold

The British Museum Catalogues even go so far as to spell out with a Mac those authors whose names actually begin with Mc or M', expanding McPhail and M'Phail to Macphail. But the writer would certainly not recommend this practice to indexers; it seems to him to be taking liberties with the owners' names and also possibly confusing to inquirers.

A year or two ago a woman sent a letter to the London *Evening Standard* complaining about the Mcs all being mixed up with the Macs in the London telephone directories. The writer replied that this practice, which was almost universal, was helpful to the subscriber who could not remember exactly how the person concerned spelled his name. If the other method of arrangement were used, Angus McDonald, for instance, would be separated by many pages from Angus Macdonald.

Quite recently the writer was somewhat astonished upon receiving for his comments a draft code drawn up at Columbia University, New York, for use in indexes made by means of a computer. (Have any of my readers ever inspected a computer-compiled index?) What amazed him was that the code ruled that Mc and M' were to be arranged in the order of their abbreviated forms. When he protested, he was told that they are frequently found arranged as spelled in the United States, e.g., in American telephone directories (as Mr. Collison has told us), some libraries, and some indexes. It should be noted, however, that under Mc in the American directories the user is told to look also under Mac.

*Saints.* Similarly the abbreviation "St" as part of a name is treated in an index as if spelled out in full—S-A-I-N-T. Thus:

Sails
Saint-Amand, Robert
*St. George and the Dragon* (title)
St. James's Square
St. John, Robert
St. Moritz
St. Paul's Cathedral

Ste Anne's Church
Sainte-Beuve, Charles Augustin
*Saints and Sinners*

Please note the position of St. Moritz. "St" here really stands for "Sankt," but only a pigheaded pedant would look for St. Moritz after all the other "Sts," and "Stes," where strictly it should be.

Please note, too, that individual saints' names should be inverted and come under the letter with which their Christian name starts. Thus:

| | |
|---|---|
| Anne, Ste | Thomas Aquinas, St. |
| James, St. | Thomas à Becket, St. |
| John the Baptist, St. | Thomas More, St., *see* More, Sir Thomas |
| Paul, St. | |

## Compound Headings

Compound groups of words (whether hyphened or not) are indexed under the initial letter of the first element of the compound, except where usage favors inversion. A little while ago the writer was astonished to see in an otherwise excellent index the following entry:

Smith, Sheila Kaye-, q. on reading, 35

The name of this well-known Sussex authoress must have occurred in countless indexes and encyclopedias, and this must be the first occasion on which it was listed under Smith, where not one reader in a hundred would think of looking for it. No special usage could cause the inversion of the surname of:

Kaye-Smith, Sheila

Unhyphenated proper names sometimes present a greater problem (e.g., Bonar Law and Lloyd George. See Chapter 4 on NAME HEADINGS, p. 63, footnote). But these can usually be solved by the use of cross references.

It is now time to deal with an important topic in alphabetical arrangement and one not unfraught with controversy. There are two systems, both in fairly general use:

**49**

the word-by-word method and the letter-by-letter. The indexer will have to decide before he starts indexing which system to use, and then to use it consistently throughout the index. He should also indicate in a preliminary note exactly what method he chose.

First, let us examine the difference between the two systems and give examples of each. A compound heading can be indexed either as a group of separate words each alphabetized in turn (the word-by-word system) or it can be treated as a single entity alphabetized all through (the letter-by-letter system). The alphabetical order may differ considerably according to which method is chosen. Examples: (from B.S. 3700)

| WORD-BY-WORD | LETTER-BY-LETTER |
|---|---|
| New Castle (Pa., U.S.A.) | Newark |
| New Haven (Conn., U.S.A.) | Newcastle (N.S.W., Australia) |
| New Testament | New Castle (Pa., U.S.A.) |
| New York | Newels |
| Newark | New Haven (Conn., U.S.A.) |
| Newcastle (N.S.W., Australia) | Newhaven (England) |
| Newels | New Testament |
| Newhaven (England) | Newton, Sir Isaac |
| Newton, Sir Isaac | New York |
| | |
| Stock Exchange | Stockerau (Austria) |
| Stock market | Stock Exchange |
| Stockerau (Austria) | Stockholm |
| Stockholm | Stock market |
| Stockport | Stockport |

*Hyphened Compounds.* The British Standard[4] revisers have decided that "words joined by hyphens shall be arranged as separate words, the hyphens being treated as spaces for filing purposes." In so deciding they have effected an alteration in the practice hitherto under the word-by-word system, under which the parts of a compound word counted as one word when one element was a prefix (or suffix) unable to stand alone.

So "post-Biblical," "pre-Cambrian," and "stand-in" will each have to be reckoned as two separate words in indexing.

[4]*Alphabetical Arrangement* (B.S. 1749:1951).

On the other hand, letter-by-letter alphabetization should not be affected by the new rule.

*Compound Abbreviations.* These, unlike the simple abbreviations already dealt with, are affected by the choice between word-by-word order and the letter-by-letter order. They consist of a compound heading comprising either one or more abbreviated words (such as *nem. con.*) or else a set of initial letters (such as B.B.C.). Sometimes the latter are pronounced and written as one word (e.g., UNESCO or Aslib), in which case they should be so indexed under either system. But otherwise, in the word-by-word system each letter of the set of initials counts as a separate word and all such groups will come (in alphabetical sequence) at the beginning of the letter concerned:

| WORD-BY-WORD | | LETTER-BY-LETTER |
|---|---|---|
| m. | [meter] | m. |
| M.A.E.E. | [Marine Aircraft Experimental Establishment] | MADAM |
| | | M.A.E.E. |
| M/C | [Marginal Credit] | MAGGI |
| M.G.M. | [Metro-Goldwyn-Meyer] | Maser |
| M.I.D.A.S. | [Measurement Information and Data Analysis System] | M/C |
| | | MEDLARS |
| M.I.T. | [Massachusetts Institute of Technology] | M.G.M. |
| | | Mgr. |
| MADAM | [Manchester Automatic Digital Machine] | MIDAS |
| | | M.I.D.A.S. |
| MAGGI | [Million Ampère Generator] | M.I.T. |
| Maser | [Microwave amplification by stimulated emission of radiation] | Mn. |
| | | *Mrs. Beeton* |
| MEDLARS | [Medical Literature Analysis and Retrieval System] | |
| Mgr. | [Monseigneur] | |
| MIDAS | [Missile Defence Alarm System] | |
| Mn. | [manganese] | |
| *Mrs. Beeton* | | |

Earlier it was mentioned that the two systems (word-by-word and letter-by-letter) are the subject of controversy among indexers, and at this stage the writer had better declare his own position. He is and has always been a fervent and unrepentant word-by-worder.

When the *British Standard of Alphabetical Arrangement* was prepared in 1951 it was taken for granted that the word-by-word principle—which it also alluded to as nothing-before-something—would be followed, except in the case of proper names starting with a definite article or preposition, such as De la Mare, Walter; De la Rue; Du Maurier, Daphne; La Fontaine, Jean de. Then followed the American Standards Association's Report in 1958, which stated that the word-by-word method of alphabetizing (New York before Newark) should be used rather than the letter-by-letter method. However it did recognize that the latter method is widely used and suggested that a note stating which method was used should be included in any given index. The Documentation Committee of the British Standards Institution, when it came to compile B.S. 3700, was quite prepared to follow suit; but when its draft report was circulated among the whole body of membership of the Society of Indexers for comment, a clamor arose from a small section of vociferous letter-by-letterists.

They protested, for instance, that, if the *Oxford Atlas* were to adopt the word-by-word system, there would be a hundred and two other names between New Haven and Newhaven, and in the case of the *Encyclopaedia Britannica* the two places would be separated by ten or eleven columns. Well, what of it? These places are entirely distinct and have no connection with each other.

The most potent argument in favor of the letter-by-letter principle used to be that it fixed compound headings in a static position, whereas hyphened words tend to develop into one word (e.g., "cut-throat" has become "cutthroat") and so alter their order under the word-by-word system. And this argument is all the stronger, seeing that for the benefit of computer programmers the revisers of the *British Standard of Alphabetical Arrangement* have decreed (see page 50) that words joined by a hyphen shall in future be treated as if separate words.

The letter-by-letter principle is chiefly used in encyclopedias (both in text and index) and gazetteers, although the

*Encyclopedia Americana* index is arranged word-by-word. It is rarely employed in ordinary literary indexes.

But the Documentation Committee took fright and in the final form of the Standard gave equal prominence to both principles. They even went further and, despite a vigorous protest from the writer, who happened to be a member, they put first all the examples of letter-by-letter.

For my part I regard the word-by-word method as far the more logical and satisfactory, particularly since it allows for all abbreviated sets of initials to come at the beginning of each letter. I strongly recommend that the indexer adopt the word-by-word principle in any indexes he may compile, unless expressly ordered to use the other. But whichever method is chosen, one must beware of describing them as something-before-nothing or nothing-before-something. It is not easy to remember which denotes what, or to understand why.

## Homonyms as Headings

Now we come to the question of indexing homonyms: two or more words or expressions having the same appearance but different meanings. Such words or expressions should invariably be made separate headings. Otherwise one will find oneself committing such egregious errors as (both examples from actual indexes):

| | |
|---|---|
| *Mill on Liberty* | Lamb and Coleridge |
| ——— *the Floss, The* | ——— mint sauce |

The order prescribed by both the British Standard of Indexing and the American Standard Basic Criteria is as follows:

1. Person or organization
2. Place
3. Subject (other than a name)
4. Title of a work, journal, etc.

Examples:

> Wells, H. G.
> Wells (Somerset)
> Wells, siting and sinking of
> *Wells:* A Report

If there are several entries in any one category, they are differentiated among themselves by descriptions and arranged alphabetically or, in the case of forenames, sometimes hierarchically, as will be explained.

> London, Charlotte, *see* London, Mrs. Jack
> London, Jack (novelist)
> London, Mrs. Jack
> London, Robert (architect)
> London, England:
>    history of
>    topography of
>    what to see and do in
> London, Ontario
> London Library
> London, Midland and Scottish Railway
> London School of Economics
> *London:* a poem

*Personal Homonyms.* With these, forenames (with titles or appellations only) precede surnames. The former may be treated either in alphabetical or in hierarchic order:

| ALPHABETICAL | HIERARCHIC |
|---|---|
| John, Archduke | John, Saints |
| John, Count | John, Pope |
| John, Emperor | John, King |
| John, King | John, Emperor |
| John, Pope | John, Archduke |
| John, Saints | John, Count |
| John, Augustus | John, Augustus |
| John, Sir William | John, Sir William |

*Homonyms of Places and Geographic Features.* It is suggested that these be indexed in gazetteer order, that is:

1. Cities and towns (with region and/or country in parenthesis)
2. Administrative areas (county, province, state, etc.)
3. Physical feature appellations (Bay, Cape, Island, Lake, River, etc.—often abbreviated)

These should all be arranged alphabetically according to the spelling of the word immediately following the homonym:

Victoria (B.C., Canada)
Victoria (Hong Kong)
Victoria, co. (Canada)
Victoria Isle (Canada)
Victoria Lake (Africa)
Victoria Lake (Australia)
Victoria River (Australia)
Victoria State (Australia)

*Subject Homonyms* (*other than proper names*). These are differentiated by description in parentheses and are arranged alphabetically according to the order of those qualifying expressions:

Pipes (conduit)
Pipes (musical)
Pipes (smokers')

Races (ethnology)
Races (hydraulics)
Races (shaft bearings)
Races (sports)

*Homonym Titles.* When titles of works or publications are identical, they are differentiated and arranged alphabetically by name of author or sponsor or place of publication added in parentheses:

*Old Wives' Tale* (Bennett—novel)
*Old Wives' Tale* (Heywood—play)

*Natura* (Amsterdam)
*Natura* (Bucharest)
*Natura* (Milan)

The last three are periodicals.

For Practical Exercises, see next two pages.

## Practical Exercises

Arrange in alphabetical order (on a separate sheet of paper) the expressions in the following lists as if compiling an index:—

(a) according to the word-by-word principle
(b) according to the letter-by-letter principle

To save time, only the number need be quoted. The solutions will be found on pages 198–199.

*Exercise 1.*[5]

(1)   *A Man for All Seasons*
(2)   Man Friday
(3)   *The Man Who was Thursday*
(4)   Man, Alfred B.
(5)   Mann & Co.
(6)   Man-eating tigers
(7)   Man-of-war
(8)   Manitoba
(9)   Mangoes
(10)  Man and wife, games partnerships of
(11)  *Man in the Iron Mask, The*
(12)  Mansfield
(13)  Mansfield, Earl of
(14)  Man-made fiber
(15)  Manning, Director of R.A.F.
(16)  *Mansfield Park*
(17)  Manningtree
(18)  Manpower
(19)  *Man and Superman*
(20)  Manorbier
(21)  Man, Isle of
(22)  Mantua
(23)  Manhattan
(24)  Manjrekar, V.
(25)  *The Man from Blankley's*
(26)  Manzanares

[5]Adapted from examples by G. V. Carey (*The Indexer*, Vol. 3, p. 95).

*Exercise 2.*

Arrange in alphabetical order the following expressions as if compiling an index:

(1) The Rev. Robert South
(2) Robert Southey
(3) South-East Asia Command
(4) South-West African Mandate
(5) The Southern Railway
(6) Victor R. Southern
(7) South America
(8) The South African War
(9) The South Pole
(10) Joanna Southcott's box
(11) Southsea Pier
(12) The South Sea Bubble
(13) Southport
(14) Southend-on-Sea
(15) Southampton
(16) Borough of Southall
(17) Borough of Southwark
(18) South Georgia
(19) South Carolina
(20) The Southern Cross
(21) *South Wind*

## 4

# *NAME HEADINGS*

E. E. G. L. SEARIGHT, C.B.E., M.C.

First, to sound a note of caution: it is important to draw distinctions between an index, a catalogue, and a gazetteer. An index is an essential, but very often not a massive part of a book, enabling the reader to find in that book the person, place, event, in which he is interested. A catalogue (especially one of the contents of a large library or a museum) or a gazetteer of a large atlas will be relatively much bigger and will certainly contain a vast number of names, names that must be readily distinguished from or related to others.

For example, in many indexes a single entry of "Stalin, Josef V." would be sufficient. In others it might be necessary to include references to his real name (Joseph V. Djugushavali) and possibly also to the first pseudonym that he adopted, i.e., "Koba."[1]

Similarly, there will be occasions when a single entry of "El Greco" will be adequate, but others when a reference to this artist's real name of Domenikos Theotokopoulos would be essential.

Again, an entry of "Salisbury" may be perfectly adequate in some indexes: in others it may be necessary to enter "Salisbury (England)" to differentiate it from "Salisbury (Rhodesia)."

[1]In 1901. He did not use the pen name of Stalin until 1913.

Let us consider names of persons first, and later, names of places.[2]

## Names of Persons

First it may be helpful to consider how names have evolved over the years and are still evolving. Here the writer is going to oversimplify—a very dangerous thing to do.

Originally a person had a personal name only, like John or Abdul. Later, as populations increased and people circulated more, it was found necessary to add a qualifying word or name. This might indicate a personal characteristic or a trade or a relationship to another person or a connection with a certain place. Here are a few examples: Eric the Red; Harun al Rashid (Harun the rightly guided); John the Smith; Thomas the Tailor; Leif Ericsson; Alexei Ivanovich; Henry Clarkson; Omar Ibn Ibrahim el Khayyam (Omar the son of Ibrahim the Tentmaker); and so on. Similarly, the late Alhadji Sir Abubakar Tafawa Balewa adopted the surname of Tafawa Balewa since that was the name of his native village. Some of these additional names were perpetuated as surnames or patronymics.

In course of time many countries adopted a stable system of surnames. China and the West have used them for a long time; Japan adopted them in 1870, Thailand between 1911 and 1925, Persia from 1921, and Turkey between 1935 and 1936.

Some nationals still never use anything but a personal name, sometimes qualified, for example in Islamic names, by relationships to father, son, or place. There is, however, an ever-increasing tendency for these people to "keep up with the Joneses" and to use the last name of their personal

[2]It may be helpful to list here some of the reference books that will be useful in identifying persons and places. *Who's Who*; *Who's Who in America*; *Who Was Who*; *International Who's Who*; *The Statesman's Year Book*; *Webster's Biographical Dictionary*; *Whitaker's Almanack*; *The Times Atlas of the World* gazetteer; Rand McNally *World Atlas*.

names as a surname. The press and public opinion contribute to this custom and so we find that Mohammed bin Othman al Said is often referred to in the press as Mr. Othman, that Mohammed Ali Khan is referred to as Mr. M. A. Khan, and Moti Singh as Mr. M. Singh.

Before indexing a person's name one should determine whether the name used is a pseudonym, a nickname, or a change of name, because persons in such categories must be treated in a special way. Sometimes the determination is easy: Saki, Sapper, Fougasse are obvious pseudonyms. But Mark Twain and George Eliot look like real names though they are in fact completely fictitious[3]. Again Daphne Du Maurier is Lady Browning's maiden name; while Agatha Christie, whose maiden name was Miller, married first a Colonel Christie and as a writer retained his name although she is now Mrs. Mallowan. (Incidentally, she also wrote under the name of Mary Westmacott, an entirely fictitious pseudonym.)

Very often a person, usually an artist, is known universally by a nickname: Jacopo Robusti as Tintoretto; Tiziano Vecelli as Titian; Claude Gelée as Claude Lorrain.

Here one must use discretion about following the cataloguing rules. The writer recommends entering the person under the form that is best known to readers, with cross references from other versions where necessary.

Allied to this question of pseudonym and nickname is the question of change of name. Pablo Picasso's father was José Ruiz Blasco; his mother was Maria Picasso Lopez. Therefore, his correct name is Pablo Ruiz Picasso with Ruiz as the operative entry name. (Spanish matronymics will be dealt with more fully later on p. 64) However, probably because he did not want to be confused with his father who was not as good an artist, he adopted the name of Pablo Picasso or sometimes Ruiz Pablo Picasso, with Picasso the operative surname.

---

[3] Samuel Langhorne Clemens, who had once been a Mississippi pilot, adopted the pen name of Mark Twain as being the phonetic rendering of the leadsman's call on the Mississippi. George Eliot was actually Miss Mary Ann Evans.

There are more examples: André Maurois was originally Emile Hertzog; Le Corbusier was named Charles-Edouard Jeanneret-Gris and in fact as an artist went by that name between 1918 and 1928. Many contemporary Frenchmen adopted fictitious names during the Resistance movement and have continued to use them since; for example, Gilbert Renault-Roulier became known during the Resistance as Colonel Remy, by which name he is still usually known.

In these cases the same treatment is recommended as was suggested for pseudonyms and nicknames.

Titles, terms of address, and honorifics should always be subordinated to the person's name, and no self-respecting indexer would dream of using the words Maître, Mr., Sir, or Viscount as key words (except as part of the title of a book). One must, however, remember that almost every country has its own titles, and he should learn to recognize these and make certain that they are subordinated to the individual's real name. This is particularly important with those persons who place their surnames first or who use a personal name only. This is not the place to give an exhaustive list of these different modes of address and titles, but here are a few examples:

| | |
|---|---|
| Burma: | Saya, Thakin, U |
| India: | Acharya, Pandit, Raja, Sri |
| Laos: | Chiao, Tiao |
| Malaysia: | Dato, Inche, Tenku, Tuanku |
| Siam (Thailand): | Luang, Mom, Nai |

Thus we see that U Thant should be indexed as "Thant, U," and Tenku Abdul Rahman as "Abdul Rahman, Tenku."

Let us now consider some special cases.

Saints, popes, kings, and princes of the blood are entered under their forenames. For example:

Stephen, Saint
John XXIII, Pope
Elizabeth II, Queen

It may sometimes be desirable to index a pope also under his name before election, using a cross reference. For example:

> Roncalli, His Eminence Cardinal Angelo Giuseppe *see* John XXIII, Pope

Other ecclesiastical dignitaries are better entered under their names and not their offices. A typical entry might be:

> Canterbury, Archbishop of, *see* Fisher, Most Rev. Geoffrey F. *and* Ramsey, Most Rev. A. Michael

provided, of course, that this office was held by both persons in the course of the volume, and both are referred to in the text.

There is one exception that the writer makes to this: he would always make his entry:

> Dalai Lama, 14th (or 5th, etc.) incarnation

unless the personal name of this dignitary before selection was mentioned in the text. In that case there should be a cross reference from that name to "Dalai Lama."

Noblemen should be entered under their titles and not under their names.[4] For example:

> Salisbury, 5th Marquess of

rather than

> Gascoyne-Cecil, Robert Arthur James, 5th Marquess of Salisbury

Surely the majority of readers would look first for Salisbury; only a few would know that Gascoyne-Cecil was the Marquess of Salisbury's family name, and of those, very few would look that name up first.

Of course with contemporary creations, or creations occurring in the course of the volume being indexed, there

---

[4]*Debrett's Peerage* and *Burke's Peerage* both list peers under their titles. The former supplies cross references from family surnames. [Editor]

must be references to both title and family name. For example:

> Lyttelton, Oliver, *see* Chandos, 1st Viscount

and

> Chandos, 1st Viscount (Oliver Lyttelton)

In these cases the writer suggests that the indexer choose for the main entry that form in which the individual is most frequently mentioned in the book or which he thinks the reader will look for first. The same procedure should naturally be followed for peers who relinquish their titles, for example, Sir Alec Douglas-Home and Mr. Quintin Hogg.

The writer always likes to pinpoint the individual by including *1st* Viscount or *14th* Earl, but with life peers this is not necessary since there will be no succession.

There are differing systems in the indexing of compound surnames: *Who's Who* follows one system; *Whitaker's Almanack* another. Personally, the writer follows British Standard 3700 and always indexes a compound hyphenated surname under the first of the compound names, e.g., Cavendish-Bentinck under C; and he follows the same practice with unhyphenated compound names if the first name is an obvious surname and not a personal name tacked on, e.g., Lloyd George[5] under L. However Chuter Ede would be entered under Ede until he inserted a hyphen by Deed Poll.

---

[5]The name "Lloyd George" has a complicated history. When the 1st Earl entered the House of Commons in 1890, it was as plain David George, and he would have been correctly indexed under G. But later the whole world was to know him as Lloyd George, and when toward the end of his life he was ennobled, he hyphened his surname in the title of Earl Lloyd-George of Dwyfor. Again, his second son, Gwilym, caused his name to be hyphenated before he entered "another place" as Lord Tenby in 1957. On the other hand the late Lady Megan, as seen in *Who's Who*, eschewed the family preference for the hyphen. It is somewhat odd to find that *Dod's Parliamentary Companion* omitted the hyphen in the case of the present earl as well as that of his sister. [Editor]

At this stage it is well to warn the reader about the custom of Spaniards and Latin Americans of Spanish origin, and of some, but not many, Portuguese, of using composite surnames, the first one being the father's surname, the second the mother's. Sometimes, but not always, a "y" is inserted between the two names. For example, Dr. Fidel Castro Ruz's father was a Castro and his mother a Ruz. Such names should always be indexed under the father's name, followed immediately by the mother's. For example:

    Castro Mendes, Mgr. Domingos

and

    Castiella y Maiz, Fernando Maria

This is not always plain sailing since the custom of using both family names is by no means universal. It is sometimes difficult to determine whether the penultimate name is, in fact, the father's surname and the last one the mother's; or whether the maternal surname has been dropped and the penultimate name is the last personal name. For example: Mgr. Domingos Castro Mendes should be indexed under C, but Sr. Cloves Luis Pestana under P.

The positioning of prefixes perhaps gives the indexer and the reader more trouble than anything else. Wherever possible, the current custom of the individual country should be followed.

Generally speaking, the practice is to index such names by the word after the one meaning "of," where this is given separately. For example:

    Brentano, Dr. Heinrich von
    Gaulle, General Charles de
    Horn, General Carl von
    Roijen, Jan Herman van

But with British and United States nationals the "des" and the "vans" and the "vons" should never be subordinated; and this applies also to nationals of the South

African Republic and Ceylon. Again, though one would rightly subordinate the "van" in a Dutch name, Achille Van Acker, a Belgian, would expect to appear among the V's.

In Islamic names the prefixes "al," "el," "ben," should be subordinated, but with Israelis the "Ben" is never so treated—therefore David Ben-Gurion appears under the B's.

Certain nationals place the surname first and the personal names after it. Chinese names are really very simple. For example, Mao Tse-tung's family name is Mao and his personal name Tse-tung; similarly Chou En-lai's family name is Chou; and they should be indexed under M and C, respectively. H. D. Talbot published an excellent article on indexing Chinese names in *The Indexer*, Vol. 2, No. 3 (1961).

The same custom obtains in Korea, Vietnam, and Cambodia, where, for example, Pho Proeung's family name is Pho and that of Norodom Sikhanouk is Norodom. It also holds in the Foulah tribe of West Africa (mainly in Guinea): Diallo Telli's surname is Diallo. Other African tribes follow the same practice: President Hamani Diori should be indexed under H and not under D.

Unfortunately for the indexer, the South Koreans (probably owing to American contacts) are now beginning to westernize their names and place the family name last. Only a year or two ago *The Times* stated that Tong Won Lee and Choong Hoeng Park were visiting this country. A couple of years before these men were normally referred to as Lee Tong Won and Park Choong Hoeng! Incidentally the numerous South Korean generals who keep on intruding into politics still stick to the traditional order of names.

In Southeast Asia, especially in South Vietnam, Laos, and Cambodia, celebrities are customarily referred to by one of their personal names only. The late president of South Vietnam was almost always spoken of as President Diem. Diem was one of that gentleman's personal names; his family name was Ngo and his full name Ngo Dinh Diem. Again, South Vietnam's present Prime Minister is

Air Vice-Marshal Nguyen Cao Ky, but he is almost invariably referred to as "Marshal Ky." Similarly Phoui Sananikone is universally known in Laos as Thao (Mr.) Phoui, and Nai (Mr.) Pridi Panomyong of Thailand as Nai Pridi. Here are cases where cross references are essential.

Besides those already mentioned, many other nationals have readily distinguishable surnames. Dr. Jafar Sharif Emami (modern Persian) is correctly indexed under Emami; the late Adnan Menderes (modern Turk) under Menderes; Tom Mboya (of Kenya) under Mboya; Moise Tshombe (of the Congo) under Tshombe; Fulbert Youlou (of Congo-Brazzaville) under Youlou; and Hayato Ikeda (of Japan) under Ikeda.

Similarly with the Siamese (Thai) and Laotians the last name is the family name. Thanat Khoman (of Siam) should be indexed as "Khoman, Thanat" and Phoui Sananikone (of Laos) as "Sananikone, Phoui."

## Islamic Names

The presentation of Islamic names can give the indexer a rare headache. Since the Islamic world stretches from Indonesia to Mauritania and embraces countries of very different races and at varying stages of culture and sophistication, this is understandable.

The *Cataloguing Rules: Author and Title Entries* published by the Library Association lays down in paragraph 52: "Arabic and other writers living in Mohammedan countries and following Mohammedan practice, are to be entered under the personal name, followed by the names expressing relationships. . . . References are to be made from each of the various names. . . . Exceptions are to be made where a name other than the personal name more readily distinguishes the author or where a particular form of the name has become established. . . ."

All right as far as it goes, but these are *cataloguing* rules, not *indexing* rules, and few indexers can afford the space for "references . . . from each of the various names."

Let us knock off the easy ones. Do not worry about Indonesian names: the operative word is nearly always an Indonesian name such as Sukarno, Nasution, and so on, sometimes with a Mohammedan name (such as Ahmed or Abdul) prefixed but which should always be subordinated.

Then there are the Persian and Turkish names. These are nearly all made up of a personal name followed by a surname, and should be indexed under the surname, e.g., "Aram, Abbas"; "Mansur, Hassan Ali."

The Mohammedans of India and Pakistan can be tricky. Most start off life with a personal name only, but find it necessary or desirable to adopt a surname. For example, Khan Bahadur (an honorific) Sharbat Khan was always Sharbat Khan, but his son Monawar Khan adopted his tribal name of Afridi as a surname and is correctly indexed as "Afridi, Monawar Khan." Similarly Ayub Khan should be indexed or referred to as "Ayub Khan," but Mohammed Ali Vakil as "Vakil, Mohammed Ali." (Vakil means lawyer and is an adopted surname.)

The Malay sticks to his personal name, qualifying it by a relationship, for example, Abdul Razak bin Hussein. Therefore Malays should be indexed under their personal names.

The Arabs vary from the less sophisticated people of Arabia to the more westernized inhabitants of Syria, Lebanon, Tunisia, Algeria, and so on. (The classic example of an Islamic name is probably Omar ibn Ibrahim al Khayyam—Omar, the son of Ibrahim, the Tentmaker. In his own day he was probably known as *Omar* al Khayyam; but nowadays the press would probably state: "The celebrated Persian poet Mr. Khayyam arrived at Heathrow today!")

The pure Arabs should be indexed under their personal names, e.g., "Faisal ibn Abdul Aziz, H. M. King of Saudi Arabia" or "Faisal ibn Hussein, H. R. H. Prince."

Generally speaking the more sophisticated Arabs should be entered under their last name, e.g., "Bella, Ahmed Ben"; "Nasser, Gamal Abdel"; "Aref, Abdul Salam Mohammed"; "Hafez, Amin el"; "Boumedienne, Col.

Houari." But again there are exceptions: that stormy petrel of Iraqi politics, Rashid Ali al Gailani, was always known as Rashid Ali and should be listed among the R's.

Hindu names add to the indexer's complications because of widely differing practices in the formation of names in different linguistic areas and among different cultural groups. For example, the caste name Rao is often used as a surname, and R. Krishna Rao might well expect to be indexed as "Rao, R. Krishna," while Mutta Venkatasubba Rao would be deeply offended if he were not set down as "Venkatasubba Rao, Mutta." Again one finds a father and his son with the former expecting to be listed as "Ayyar, Mangudy Visbanatha" and the latter as "Subrahmanyan, Mangudy." And another member of the Ayyar caste would be correctly indexed as "Ramaswami Ayyar, C. P."

The present president of the All-India Congress Party, Kumaraswami Kamaraj, should be indexed under Kamaraj; yet a few years ago when he was Chief Minister of Madras he was known as Kamaraj Nadar (Nadar being a caste name) and was correctly listed under Nadar.

As stated earlier, Acharya is an honorific—yet one will find it sometimes used as a surname, as Vinoba Bhave Acharya and Laxmi Raman Acharya, both properly indexed under A.

On the whole, the safest indexing would use the last name, although there are certain very important exceptions. Sometimes a word in the name is complementary to the name immediately before it and should never be used as a surname or family name: Shiv Prasad and Gopi Chand are examples. Basically it is incorrect to refer to the late President of India as President Prasad rather than President Rajendra Prasad, but since the incorrect form has become so universal there should be a cross reference from Prasad.

Again, among Sikhs the personal name is usually followed by the word Singh which should always be subordinated to the personal name and never used independently as a surname, though its variant Sinha is used by many Hindus in

Bengal as a surname. Sikhs sometimes use clan names as surnames: Ahluwalia, Garewal, Sethi are examples. In such cases they should be listed under the clan name, followed by the personal name. Example:

Gyani, Major-General Prem Singh

For those interested in the subject of Indic names, an article entitled "Rendering of Indic names in catalogue entries" by Benoyendra Sengupta, published in *Indian Librarian*, Vol. 13, No. 3 (1958), is well worth study.

A Burmese name should be entered in full without inversion followed by the term of address. Examples:

U Ba U should be indexed as Ba U, U

and

Daw Mya Shein as Mya Shein, Daw

The majority of Tibetan names that come the way of an indexer contain an element indicative of an office held or an honorific title; place names of monasteries or districts occur frequently; family names not infrequently; personal names less frequently. The indexer should attempt whenever possible to list an individual under his family name; if this is impossible, then under the name of his district or monastery; or, failing these, his personal name.

Another complication concerns prelates, monk officials connected with the administration of the great monasteries, monk and lay officials of the government, and lesser officials, all of whom have their own series of titles. Sometimes these are combined with the name of a monastery, sometimes with a family name, sometimes with a personal name. Which name is to be placed first or last varies with the type of office and class of person. For further light on this subject see a note by the writer in *The Indexer*, Vol. 3, No. 2 (1962).

A word now about alphabetical arrangement of names. When an article or preposition is given in the entry word at the beginning of a name, the whole name should be arranged as if it were a single word. Example:

| | | |
|---|---|---|
| Desai | | de Silva |
| de Silva | *not* | de Valera |
| de Valera | | Desai |
| Devitt | | Devitt |

Similarly with Irish names beginning with O or O'. Example:

Obote
O'Brien
Odinga
O Donnell
O'Donovan

Prefixes to names, such as "Mac" or "Saint," which may occur in contracted forms, should be arranged as if spelled in the fullest form. Example:

| | |
|---|---|
| McAdden | Saidi |
| MacArthur | St. Clair |
| Macaulay | Saint Hillier |
| M'Bain | St. Laurent |
| McCallum | Saiti |
| Macdonald | Sakata |

But, though M'Bain may be a contracted form of Mac-Bain, African names such as M'Ba are not contractions of MacBa, and should take their normal place—in the case of M'Ba between Mazowiecki and Mbanefo.

## Names of Places

Bentley said, "Geography is about Maps, but Biography is about Chaps." Let us now finish with chaps and consider maps, or rather places.

What the indexer must always remember is that his entry must never leave the user in doubt as to what place is referred to, especially when there are two or more of the same name.

As stated earlier, indexes that call for geographic names as key words vary considerably. They range from those with very few such entries (and those probably so obvious that further description may be redundant), through indexes to books on travel or history in which a considerable number of places are mentioned, right up to a gazetteer, when the most complete definition possible is essential. The indexer must use his discretion, but follow the general rule: "When in doubt, amplify."

First of all comes the choice of the key word. In the index to a recently published book, "People's Republic of China" is found among the P's. The writer would have entered it as "China, People's Republic of."

Where a country is divided into two geographical parts one preference is for the entry word to be the name of the country, for example:

    Vietnam, North
    Vietnam, South

and

    Korea, North
    Korea, South

When, however, the two parts are long-established separate entities, the order should be reversed, for example:

    North Carolina
    South Carolina

With cities, towns, counties, *arrondissements*, states, provinces, and departments, the name of the place should be followed by the name of country, and then by any further description necessary. Examples:

    Alexandria (Egypt)
    Alexandria (Scotland)
    Cork, Ireland (city)
    Cork, Ireland (county)

Two or more places of the same name in a given country or state should be distinguished by the addition of the names of the province, department, county, and so on. Examples:

    Bradford, Eng. (Devonshire)
    Bradford, Eng. (Northumberland, Berwick-upon-Tweed div.)
    Bradford, Eng. (Northumberland, Wansbeck div.)
    Bradford, Eng. (Yorkshire)

Rivers, unlike towns, tend to wander through several states or counties—sometimes even countries. Rivers of the same name in a given country would probably best be distinguished by the addition of the county, state, etc., with which they are most usually associated, followed by "etc."

Take the word "Avon." Apart from a French town and a Scottish loch of that name, there are two rivers in Scotland, four in England, nine in the United States, and two in Australia and New Zealand bearing the name of Avon. There may be dozens more!

Of the English Avons, one flows through Devonshire; one flows through Bradford-on-Avon (Wiltshire), Bath (Somerset), and, after passing through Bristol (Gloucestershire), into the Severn at Avonmouth; another runs through Salisbury (Wiltshire) and enters the sea at Christchurch (Hampshire); the fourth moves through Stratford-on-Avon (Warwickshire) to join the Severn in Worcestershire.

Recommended index entries for these four rivers are:

    Avon, river, Eng. (Devonshire)
    Avon, river, Eng. (Gloucestershire)
    Avon, river, Eng. (Hampshire)
    Avon, river, Eng. (Warwickshire)

Since there is probably only one River Thames in England, at most one would need to enter it as: "Thames, river, England," and England need be mentioned only if one wished to distinguish it from two other rivers of the same name, one in Connecticut and one in Ontario.

Some rivers change their names through their courses. The Brahmaputra is called thus in India and East Pakistan, but is known as the Tsangpo in Tibet. In such cases one should enter it under the better known name or under the one used more frequently in the text, with cross references from the other.

The names of places often change, especially in these days of emergent states and turnovers of regimes. The Gold Coast became Ghana; the French Sudan, the Republic of Mali. The Irish harbor of Dunleary was renamed Kingstown in honor of King George IV when he landed there in 1821; in 1921 it reverted to Dun Laoghaire (same pronunciation as, but different spelling from, its original name). St. Petersburg became Petrograd and later Leningrad; Danzig is now called Gdansk; Tsaritsyn was first renamed Stalingrad and now Volgograd. How the indexer should treat such places depends to a great extent on the text being indexed, always using a cross reference when in doubt.

Generally speaking, geographic names used as key words should be given in the English form. Examples:

> Munich, not München
> Austria, not Oesterreich

However, the text of the book will give the indexer guidance in this matter, although the latter should always consider the possibility of a reader looking for the entry under some other form. If he has any doubts he should make two entries, one being a cross reference.

## Alphabetical Order

As regards compound names, the indexer can choose between the word-by-word method and the letter-by-letter method of alphabetical arrangement. The writer recommends the former system (e.g., New York in front of Newcastle). But this whole topic has been fully dealt with in the preceding chapter (ALPHABETICAL ARRANGEMENT), which the reader is advised to consult.

In conclusion, it cannot be emphasized too strongly that the indexer's function is to help the reader find references to a person or a place as quickly as possible, and therefore he must project himself constantly into the probable index-user's mind.

## Practical Exercise

The indexer is working on a contemporary autobiography. Among the names worthy of an entry in the index are the following. How should they be presented? For solutions see pages 199–200.

1. Marshal Chen Yi (China)
2. Lord Attlee (U.K.)
3. Nai Sawat Mahapol (Siam)
4. President Eamon de Valera (Eire)
5. Hugo le Gallais (France)
6. General Carl von Horn (Sweden)
7. Walter de la Mare (U.K.)
8. Rinaldo Del Bo (Italy)
9. H. M. King Paul I of the Hellenes
10. Manzur Qadir (Pakistan)
11. Pieter van Rooy (Netherlands)
12. César Pachero Batlle (Uruguay)
13. Rt. Hon. Clement Richard Attlee (U.K.)
14. William R. van Straubenzee (U.K.)
15. General François de Clerc (France)
16. Rt. Rev. A. Mervyn Stockwood, Bishop of Southwark
17. Hashim Jawad (Iraq)
18. Sardar Swaran Singh (India)
19. Dr. Antonio de Oliveira Salazar (Portugal)
20. Sr. Don Gabriel Arias Salgado (Spain)
21. Rt. Hon. W. David Ormsby-Gore (U.K.)
22. Kham Sing Gonvorath (Laos)
23. Inche Suleiman bin Dato Abdul Rahman (Malaya)
24. Thakim Tin Maung (Burma)
25. Giorgio La Pira (Italy)
26. Gopal Krishna Gokhale (India)
27. Sheikh Abdul Aziz ibn Hassan (Saudi Arabia)

# 5

# SUBJECT HEADINGS

DEREK LANGRIDGE[1]

## Fundamental Principles

In this discussion I shall use the term "book indexing" to mean the indexing of individual works, as distinct from collections.

A vast amount of literature now available deals with all aspects of the indexing of collections, but most of the literature on book indexing concentrates on the less difficult problems; while the fundamental problems of how to make the subject entries and how to choose them are not treated very well. In an article contributed to the *Sayers Memorial Volume*, published by the Library Association in 1960, I attempted to indicate how these problems can be solved.

There are two similar activities to be considered: one is the indexing, the input stage, and the other is the searching, the user's side. The indexer deals with a document written in the *author's* own natural language. The searcher puts his inquiry in *his* own natural language. The indexer must translate or reduce the document into *indexing* language. The searcher (or user) has to try to answer his inquiry by examining the indexer's language. The indexing language refers to a store of materials, which might be a library, a periodical, a book, or any other sort of collection.

[1]I wish to stress the fact that this chapter is an edited version of a lecture and not a specially written paper. D. L.

## The Nature of Subjects

The first question is: "What is a subject?" If one takes the book, *How to Sell Successfully by Direct Mail*, there are two extreme ways of dealing with it. One is represented by the basic library operation: an attempt to tell what the total contents of the book are; this method will be referred to as summarization. A summarization as used in libraries would probably reduce the subject of the book mentioned to three words "Direct Mail Advertising." The other extreme tries to give all the topics covered by the book. It is represented by the book's own index which consists, in this case, of several hundred entries. This method is known as extraction, or exhaustive indexing. All indexing lies somewhere between the two extremes. If an index is to go in the book, it is compiled by exhaustive indexing, a listing of *all* the concepts in the book. If the total content of the book is merely summarized, exhaustive indexing is not being practiced. "Exhaustivity" or "depth of indexing" are the terms used for this concept. The other important concept in indexing policy is specificity. Whatever the degree of exhaustivity in indexing, each concept can be treated more or less specifically. The summarization of the previously mentioned book as "Direct Mail Advertising" is the most specific way in which the total content can be described; but it might be described more generally as "Advertising," or "Marketing." Both of these descriptions would be true; but they would not be specific. This is not a book covering the whole field of marketing or advertising; it covers only direct mail advertising. These ways of describing the whole book are three successive stages of specifying, but only "Direct Mail Advertising" is a specific description of the entire content of the book. In the same way, any of the concepts in a book index can be expressed more or less specifically. For example, one might merely put the entry "Accountants." On the other hand, to make clear what that entry says about accountants, it might be made to read "Accountants as market."

The policy regarding exhaustive indexing rests largely on economics. It depends on how much money is available for indexing, on what staff there is, and on what other things one must do with that staff, and on the sort of inquiries that come in. If users only want to identify items by their general content, then there is no point in exhaustive indexing. Take an ordinary public library as an example. Obviously it could never attempt what is done in the book indexing, for that would be beyond the bounds of economic feasibility, and on the whole public libraries are forced by conditions to limit themselves to describing whole books. They do go a bit beyond this if there is a chapter, or a part of the book, that is not obviously included in the general description. Then an extra entry may be made, thus leaning a little toward exhaustivity. In special libraries, where the field of study is narrower, more exhaustive indexing is economically possible. In any special library, one usually finds more analytical entries for the books than in public libraries; and in a special information service that is dealing with really detailed information, one may find at least a part of that collection quite exhaustively indexed. Company reports, for example, may well be indexed in detail, though perhaps not in so much detail as a book. There may well be twenty entries for a report, instead of the one or two found in the usual library.

Specificity depends to some extent on the size of the index, but on the whole very little can be said for anything other than specific indexing. Consistency is very difficult with unspecific indexing; and if it is used because the collection is small at the moment, time is likely to change conditions. A fundamental law of library science is that a library is a growing organism—and here "library" applies to any form of collection. What may well do for sorting out documents now, may be hopelessly inadequate in two, three, five, or ten years time. One of the worst things to cope with is the indexing of a collection that was not adequately indexed to begin with.

The same holds true of indexing books. One is sometimes

told that there is no need to go into specific detail in making the entries in books. But suppose that there is an entry for the "Army" in a book on the business of management. Is it not worth while showing precisely what that entry is about, to save a user not interested in that aspect from wasting his time turning up the reference? If the entry reads "Army, marketing by," then the person looking for information on army organization need not follow up the reference.

In dealing with periodicals, either of the two extremes of summarization and exhaustive indexing is possible. What may be needed on the one hand is merely a record which summarizes the whole of the contents of each article, or, on the other hand, an exhaustive index which goes into great detail. Here again the decision is a matter of the use to which the periodical is going to be put, and of the economics of the affair. The two things have to be balanced. Obviously one can do only what one's economics allow, even if more would be worth while; but the important thing is to decide first what *ought* to be done and only secondly what *can* be. If you know what *ought* to be done, you can make a stronger case for any extra staff or money required.

## Word Indexing and Concept Indexing

The next important distinction to be made is that between word indexing and concept indexing. It is possible to index documents merely by using the words that appear in them. There are some indexes which use only the titles of books for the purpose of description. This is word indexing, and its advantages are fairly obvious. It can be done by unskilled labor; it can be easily mechanized; and it can be done quickly. Having said this, nothing more can be said for it; it is the crudest possible form of indexing, and in very few circumstances is it worth doing.

There is a vogue at the moment for the "KWIC Index," (Key-word-in-context). These indexes take the titles of periodical articles and arrange them by the key words in the title, so that each key word features as an entry in the alphabetical arrangement. The indexes can be produced extremely quickly, and therefore are of some value for what is called current awareness services—that is, they can inform specialists very early of new material appearing in their fields. A completely inexperienced person compiling an alphabetical index to a book might get a similar result merely by taking words from the text without relating synonyms or showing any other kinds of relations.

Concept indexing, on the other hand, recognizes the subject, in whatever words it is expressed, and then chooses the word or words by which to express it. Concept indexing needs a controlled vocabulary. For each concept a particular word or words must be chosen and references made from other words that readers might look for.

## The Nature of Inquiries

The next question is: What is a subject inquiry? There are three kinds, though they are not completely mutually exclusive. The first is a specific request. Somebody might ask: What have you got on direct mail advertising? Second, there is a generic inquiry, in which the searcher starts at one point and then explores all the most closely related subjects. For example, he may go on from direct mail advertising to all other kinds of advertising. The third kind of inquiry, which is very common, might be called a vague inquiry, when a person has only a glimmering of what he wants. Every library worker meets this sort of question and knows he must guide the inquirer to the appropriate material. But if all that can be offered is a set of specific words arranged in alphabetical order, this is not going to get the inquirer very far. Any system of indexing which attempts to answer only specific inquiries assumes that people do not make generic inquiries. It further assumes, falsely, that subjects can be completely separated and isolated from each other, and that people are always able to define precisely what they want in the indexer's terms. This is the biggest assumption of all and is completely untrue. As

Alan Rees has pointed out, the language of an inquiry very frequently does not represent clearly formed concepts, but an attempt to *formulate a concept*. If you assume that the inquirer always formulates his concept in precise words, and that those words are used in the index, you are obviously in error.

The conclusions to be drawn from the foregoing are: merely to provide access by a list of words arranged in alphabetical order is never sufficient in any kind of indexing system; relationships must always be clearly shown; and there must be a pattern of knowledge somewhere in the system. Imagine an iceberg as representing an indexing system, with the final arrangement of the index being what shows above the water. Now this final arrangement may be an alphabetical order, a classified order, or both. In this portion one can distinguish between classification and indexing; but below the water are all the operations supporting the final arrangement. Here classification is fundamental to all kinds of indexing.

## Classification and Indexing

If the indexer is to provide a proper guide to the contents of a book, a periodical, or a collection of material, he must know what his subject includes and how the various parts are related. Book indexers may think that they know their subject well and that they do not need to worry about this classification since it is there unconsciously. To some extent, and within a limited field, this may be true. I still do not accept it, because I think that any activity is performed better if brought to the conscious level. Moreover, if you go beyond making an index for one book on one occasion, then you have the more difficult task of insuring consistency in the work. Several people may be working on the same job and there must be consistency between them. And if an indexer is working over a long period of time, he must be sure that he is consistent with himself throughout the project.

The difference between the two kinds of presentation can be illustrated by comparing an ordinary dictionary with *Roget's Thesaurus*. The first is arranged in alphabetical order, the latter by grouping together words which have similar meanings. But Roget also includes an alphabetical index through which one can locate groups of related words. If one is concerned with the meaning of a specific word, the alphabetically arranged dictionary will answer. If, on the other hand, when one is writing, a more precise word is needed than comes to mind, then an ordinary alphabetical arrangement will not help; only a thesaurus will be of real assistance. This is a simple demonstration of the fact that alphabetical arrangement, however necessary in any system, is rarely by itself sufficient.

In a library the usual system is to arrange the material itself in a classified order. A record of the material in that library is made in a catalogue. This may be a *classified* catalogue, consisting of a set of cards representing the books in a systematic sequence, plus an alphabetical index to the classification. An alternative form is the dictionary catalogue, in which *subjects* are arranged in alphabetical order with cross references. The difference between these two is that in the classified catalogue closely related subjects are kept together and in the dictionary catalogue they are separated but linked by cross references.

The systematically arranged contents of a book correspond to the systematically arranged collection in a library. The book's index corresponds to the library catalogue. Since book indexes are always alphabetically arranged they should be based on the principles of the dictionary catalogue. They should show not only the subjects in the text, but also the *relationships between subjects*.

Take, for example, the terms "management," "planning," "organizing," and "control." In an alphabetical index, these terms are separated from each other; and anybody looking up one of these words is going to find references which relate only to it, and not to the others. If the index to the book is to do an equivalent job to the library catalogue, then cross references must be made: after page references under "Management" one would have to add: "*See also* Planning; Organizing; *and* Control, and so on."

## Classification and Book Indexing

Now let us turn to the construction of an index for a book or a periodical. One has to start, if what has been said earlier is true, with a classified pattern as the basis of the work. It is easy to construct the outline of a classification scheme after one reading of the book, so long as the correct technique is understood. This is very well described in a short and lucid book by B. C. Vickery, *Faceted Classification*, published by Aslib.

The process consists of recognizing categories of terms and relationships between them. A book on export marketing will serve as an example. An examination of this book showed that the subjects fell into seven categories. There were general concepts relating to exports as a whole, such as the definition of exporting, the importance of exporting, and so on. This was one category. The second referred to the exporter, and consisted mainly of names of companies, of firms, and of individuals, or certain things that were said about individuals: the sort of career they might have in export or the sort of life they would have to lead when abroad. The third category was concerned with the markets for goods, and consisted of names of countries or groups of countries, or of descriptions of countries, such as developing ones, and of consumers, such as women or housewives. The next group of terms fell into a category of conditions, such as climate and communications in the various countries, political situations, social aspects like class and occupations of the persons in the country, and economic matters like the currency. The fifth category concerned the products that were being sold: capital goods, consumer goods, raw materials, and invisible exports. The next category covered techniques of marketing, such as advertising, distribution, market research, presentation, product study, promotion, and public relations. The final group included general business functions, such as finance, legal, production, and management.

Once having recognized the set of categories to be used, and once having entered a few words in each, the indexer can see immediately what other words are likely to appear. Then when he goes through the book he can more easily identify what is important for the index and what is not.

Some published classification schemes are constructed on this method. They do not attempt to enumerate all the subjects that could occur within a field by including all possible compound subjects. They give merely the names of the categories and the lists of elementary terms. Such a classification for a particular field of study is an enormous help, whatever form of index is being compiled.

## Compound Subjects

If one could express each concept by a single word then the job of arrangement would be easy. But most index entries consist of two or more words. At one extreme there is the possibility of permutation. If there are two terms in the subject, then the number of permutations is two; if three terms, the number is six; and if four terms, twenty-four. This kind of progression makes permutation impracticable for most purposes.

A second possible answer is a method known as rotation. This brings to the front of the entry each word in turn, so that for "Direct mail advertising," there would be one entry under "Direct mail advertising," one under "Advertising, direct mail," and one under "Mail advertising, direct." With rotation the number of entries corresponds exactly to the number of terms, and there are considerably fewer entries than with permutation. Rotation is usually adequate and suitable for book indexing, though not for indexing on a very large scale.

There is another method which is described by John Sharp in *Some Fundamentals of Information Retrieval*, published by Deutsch in 1965. He calls it "Selective listing in combination" (SLIC for short). In this system three terms, which in permutation would need six entries, would need only four. For four terms, permutation would give twenty-four entries, SLIC only eight. Obviously one can have a fair number of terms before getting beyond the bounds of economic feasibility.

## Procedure in Book Indexing

Since a pattern of knowledge underlies all the work performed in indexing, the procedure for making a book or a periodical index can be improved. The usual instructions found in books on indexing, are that, starting at the beginning of the book (having previously read it thoroughly) one makes entries on cards or slips from page 1, and files them in alphabetical order from the beginning. A better method is to start with a set of cards for categories and to file individual references in the appropriate place. In this way the job is under control the whole of the time. The categories suggest the sort of entries to be made, as well as quickly revealing omissions. By the time this operation is completed, it is possible to see what cross references are necessary. The last stage is to arrange all the entries in alphabetical order.

This method is also helpful in deciding what entries are *not* necessary. For example, if the total subject of the book is "Retailing," there is no point in making an entry under "Retailing" [except as key word of a title—Editor]: all entries would have to appear as sub-divisions.

Subjects that are used in illustration do not usually call for indexing; for the phrase "large industrial companies like I.C.I. and Unilever," no entries for I.C.I. and Unilever are needed. This eliminates any *automatic* underlining of every name in a book. The same is true for negative references, such as "There is nothing in Great Britain comparable to the Harvard Business School." Again, a reference merely to another part of the text, such as "a contribution at the end of this book on Lyons Corner Houses," would not give the slightest information on Lyons Corner Houses. Finally, the location or the audience of a speaker *may* be omitted from the index. It is doubtful whether an entry for the Australian Institute of Management is wanted for "Lord Slim, who, when lecturing not many years ago in Australia to the Australian Institute of Management, said . . ."

Great caution must be exercised, however, in deciding not to put such items in. There are so many uses to which readers put books that the indexer can never be sure that he is not overlooking some peculiar need. There may always be someone for whom a passing mention has significance. The principle should be: if there is any doubt whatever, put it in. There may be a number of ideas in a book which seem quite obvious and of which one might say, "This is in every book on the subject, what is the point of indexing it?" The indexer should never forget that for some who buy that book, it may be their only book on the subject. The index is for them as well as for others who have many books on the subject. It is important to remember that the economic balance lies between the time that it takes to make an entry (this applies not only to book indexing, but to any kind of indexing) and the time wasted by the user trying to find information that was not indexed. In other words, if the indexer is saving himself half an hour by not making a particular kind of entry, how many hours of how many other people's time is he wasting? This is always extremely difficult to estimate, but in terms of extreme cases, of books that have no indexes, how many hours of time have been wasted looking through, say biographies. Quite obviously, detail in the indexing at the input stage must be very carefully considered, because at that stage only one person's time is being spent and it is being spent once and for all.

# 6

# THE LONG INDEX

JAMES C. THORNTON

The subject of this chapter is the long index, meaning by this something which might take up as much as a volume by itself. The excuse for giving the long index a place in the present volume is that, if the student of indexing understands the principles on which a long index is compiled, he should be better equipped, not only to prepare a long index, but also to make a better job of what might without disrespect otherwise be called an ordinary index.

## When Needed

Scholarly works that embody literary or historical research, or scholarly editions of the collected works of great authors, particularly the great discursive writers such as Samuel Johnson, Coleridge, Hazlitt, or Ruskin—these must have long indexes. A short index would be inadequate and, therefore, however good the principles on which it is compiled, of necessity a bad index. But a long index is not necessarily a good index. A long bad index is very much worse than a short bad index: it is more difficult to find out how bad it is, for it takes some time and patience to discover and appraise its virtues and its vices. One must learn how an indexer's mind was working in order to know under what heads to look for the information desired. The faults of a long index are not easily apparent, but it is by studying the faults as well as the merits that an indexer can learn the best method of preparing a good index himself. The best way is to go to the best models, and learn from them the method and principles on which they were laid out. The majority of long indexes have a prefatory note; sometimes more than this. At the beginning there may be quite a little essay explaining the principles, intentions, and way of working that the indexer adopted.

How does one test an index? First, he studies the introduction that the indexer himself may have supplied to explain the scope of the index and the method followed. Then from the index itself he observes how the method worked out in practice. Another helpful step is to check related entries to see whether each is complete in itself, or whether cross references are needed, and if so, whether they are stated. To give a simple example: if under the name "Smith, A," there is a reference to a certain page to show that he was in Cardiff, the same page number should also be entered under "Cardiff," or if sufficiently important a cross reference from Cardiff to Smith.

Another test is to read a passage in the text and decide for oneself: "How would I have indexed that passage, and, second, what would I look for in the index in order to find that particular passage again." This is a very salutary exercise as well as a test of the index that is being examined.

## Indexing Masterpieces

Let us look at four masterly indexes, to which the student of indexing would do well to pin his faith. Too many rules or standards or guides, which may appear to conflict, can distract the student and sometimes actually do. So it is good practice to examine good indexes to learn the principles on which they were compiled.

The four are as follows: first, the index which occupies the whole of Volume 39 of Cook and Weddenburn's edition of Ruskin's *Works* (published in 1912). Particular attention should be given to the introduction. Second, the index to L. F. Powell's revision (1964) of Birkbeck Hill's edition of Boswell's *Life of Samuel Johnson*. Had not Powell produced his own index, the list given here would have included the one by his predecessor, Birkbeck Hill, an index produced in 1892 and one of the first major indexes that still satisfy the requirements of modern scholarship. Birkbeck Hill's contribution to the profession of indexing is his introduction of alphabetical order and categorization into the descriptive material or subheadings within each entry or article.

The third and fourth indexes on this list are R. W. Chapman's to his edition of Samuel Johnson's *Letters* (1952) and E. S. de Beer's to his edition of Evelyn's *Diary* (1955). To put these works side by side brings up the question of whether it is advisable to have one index or more than one index.

## One Index or More Than One

Powell and de Beer favor the single index, while Chapman champions the multiple index. Chapman's edition of Johnson's *Letters* in three volumes has seven classified indexes, which together occupy 135 pages of Volume III. He used his indexes as a means of conveying to the reader a good deal of information of a kind that in other editions would find its way into the annotation or into an introductory note. The multiple index in this instance is therefore a valuable editorial device. Apart from such special circumstances, the indexer of any considerable and varied work will have to decide whether to have one single alphabetical sequence to include both proper names and common nouns, or whether to divide the entries into, say, a name index and a subject index. "Subject" in this context is a conventional term to differentiate topics from proper names. (To avoid ambiguity, the word "topic" is sometimes used instead of "subject.") In a biography of the Duke of Wellington, the Duke of Wellington is the subject, but in indexing terms Wellington is a name, while his armies, his wars, and his battles are subjects or topics. If, however, the distinction between two indexes is simply that one contains proper names and the other common nouns, it may soon be found that a number of proper names must in common sense find their place in the subject index. If philosophy is a "subject," so is Platonism, although the latter is a proper noun. Therefore in a separate subject index, it is wise to restrict the accompanying index or indexes to names of persons and places. Even so, in our hypothetical life of the Duke of Wellington it will tax the indexer to decide in which index to place the Peninsular War. He may be forced to put it under "Wellington," "Spain," and "Portugal" in the person and place index, and under some general heading such as "wars" in the subject index. In the light of these difficulties it would seem that a single alphabetical sequence is convenient for the consultant and solves more problems than it creates for the indexer.

Before leaving the subject of the single versus the multiple index, one argument should be mentioned which favors the hiving-off of the subjects or topics in a separate index of their own. This is that, otherwise, a few common nouns tend to become lost among a host of personal names. The answer to this very real objection is given by de Beer in his introduction to an index where he supplies a list of the subject headings. This list is prefaced by the following paragraph:

> All subjects are entered in the general alphabetical sequence of the index. Those defined by proper names are entered under them. Those not defined by proper names are grouped, as far as possible, under general headings. The following classified list gives these headings. . . .

A great advantage of this device is that the consultant can see at a glance not only the range of the subject indexing but also the key words which have been chosen. Without this a person consulting a subject index for the first time may have to look up a number of possible words, fairly synonymous, before he finds the one which the indexer has chosen. Cross references are helpful here, but there are limits to the number that should be inserted. The indexer must therefore use great care in choosing his key word. It must be the one most likely to be looked for and most in conformity with the text. In an eighteenth-century work, for instance, a reader would be unlikely to look up the modern word "transport" if he wished for references to coaching.

After this digression on the single and multiple index, let us assume that the indexer has decided whether to have one or more indexes. Whatever he decides, he will be confronted with bulk. The distinguishing mark of the "long index" is, not surprisingly, its length, which is not, however, the result simply of having a large number of different headings as the main items of the index. Here is de Beer on this question of length:[1] "What generally differentiates indexes of books of this class (that is, scholarly editions of extensive literary or historical texts) from the indexes of shorter and more everyday books is the far more frequent presence in them of long entries: that is, entries which bring together a large number of defined references under a single general heading." By a defined reference de Beer means one in which a statement is made about the subject of the entry. That is to say, the indexer has not contented himself with entering, say, the name, "Wellington, Duke of," followed by a string of page numbers. He has also entered various phrases that will differentiate and define each of the references.

## Analysis and Synthesis

From the foregoing it follows that the indexer's first task is to analyze the text of the book he is working on, under various headings or words that will need to be grouped and regrouped and finally reduced to order. This is a twofold task. There are two separate functions: analysis and

[1] E. S. de Beer, "The Larger Index," *The Journal of Documentation* (March 1956), page 1.

synthesis. Analysis may give an author a long list of words and phrases; then comes the synthesizing function of putting them together. Powers of analysis are applied to the text; synthesis is applied to the material which the indexer has drawn from the text.

Let us deal with the analysis first. Here it is necessary to break down the author's meaning, and that is not always the same as summarizing. Not often will a single sentence summarize a whole page. More often the indexer has to represent his understanding of the author's meaning by selecting single words (or phrases) and making statements with reference to these. At this early stage analysis ought not to be the same as condensation. It is rather a disentangling process, like raveling a piece of cloth into its component parts to bring out the separate fibers and fine strands that may not appear on the surface. By this is meant that in the reading of the author's text the indexer must look for allusions which are not explicit, and for hidden references to persons or events. There are indexes where the name is entered only when it is actually mentioned in the text: that is to say, Wellington is indexed whenever the name occurs but omitted if reference was to the Iron Duke. That is an extreme example, but similar ones do happen. The indexer therefore must not overlook even more abstruse or esoteric allusions.

By the time the indexer has gone through the text and reduced it to a number of proper names and subjects that he has entered on cards, he will have a vast quantity of the latter, each containing a page number and most of them also a short descriptive phrase. If he were to take all his cards and arrange them in the order in which they were written, they would, if read through in sequence, give a fairly complete idea of the whole book. One is sometimes tempted to think that the purpose of the index is to save the trouble of reading the book. An index can do this, but admittedly this is not its prime purpose. The indexer serves not only the reader who, having read the book, wishes to refer again to some passage that he remembers or half remembers; he also caters to the person who wishes only to find out whether the book contains anything connected with a subject in which he is interested, and which he reasonably supposes might have been mentioned by the author of the book he is consulting.

The mention of these two classes of consultants brings us to the question whether the indexer should aim at completeness or selection. In thinking about what is to go into the index, he has also naturally to think in an equally positive way about what is to be left out. His conclusions will, I suggest, be different for an index of proper names than for an index of topics or subjects.

In indexing names of persons and places the ideal is to include them all, and all the references to each. If any names have to be omitted for reasons of space, they should belong to a category of names which can be specified, and the fact clearly stated at the beginning of the index. For instance, if a book contains a number of biographical footnotes for general information and without much detailed bearing on the text, it may be legitimate to say that the place-names and titles of works occurring in such notes are omitted from the index if not mentioned elsewhere. It may also be legitimate to refrain from indexing standard works of reference cited in the annotation. Omissions from the text itself are more difficult to justify. What principle of selection can the indexer impose if he is dealing with one of the great works of literature or with a work of scholarship or a compilation of learning? Is the indexer the one to say that *this* reference is important and *that* one is not? All he can say is that among various references[2] under the same head some are more important in their context than others. This he can do perfectly well, and he must do it; but it is not for him to say: "No one will bother to look up the lesser references, so I will leave them out." They should all go in and the principal references must be differentiated

2[The author here uses the term "references" sometimes in a more general sense than the strict index meaning in "Definitions of Indexing Terms" on page 12. Editor.]

from those which are less important—less important, that is to say, in their context. If there is only one reference, it should go in by virtue of the fact that there is no other.

The question of completeness or selection is not so simply answered when the index is one of topics indicated by a common noun or an adjectival phrase. The indexer has clearly to be selective unless his index is to become a concordance. He cannot, however, be guided in his selection solely by the relative importance of the various subjects as treated in the text of his author. He must know his way about the ramifications of knowledge to which his author is, or may be reasonably supposed to be, a contributor. He must have a historical imagination to perceive the interest of a subject against the background of the time in which the author was writing—even though the mention may be only a passing allusion. He must also be aware of those aspects of his author which are most prominent in the minds of readers of the present day, and he must try to forecast other aspects which may have more interest for readers of a future generation. All this is asking a good deal, and the following pointers are offered only as guidelines of what the selection of topics for indexing should include

1. Topics that are the subject of important mention by the author.

2. Topics that are important to a study of the work of the author—this, apart from general subject matter, may include words coined by the author or distinctive phrases or characteristic images.

3. Topics that are important to a student of the life of the author, or of the age in which he lived, in relation to his work—whether or not such topics are treated extensively in the text.

4. Topics that are of general or historical interest for which it is reasonable to suppose the author might be consulted if only to find out whether they receive a mention and if so to what extent.

Finally, once a topic is selected for inclusion, it is best not to be too selective, if selective at all, in listing the references to it.

It will be clear from much of what has been said above that the main part of the work of editing an index is in the assessment of the relative importance of the various references and their evaluation one against the other. Although the analyzing process, referred to earlier, may have been spread over months or even years, while reading the text and writing the index cards, the editing should be concentrated into as short a time as possible. The descriptive phrases on the cards will have been written at different times and in different moods. They will be some help in a preliminary sorting, but experience has shown that it will be generally advisable in the editing to look up most or all of the references again. A large number of references may relate to the same subject or person, twenty or thirty or more, and it is advisable to consult the text again at one sitting on each of them. This will incidentally check the accuracy of the page numbers. It will also refresh the mind: the indexer will then be able to lay the references in front of him, possibly physically, certainly mentally. This will also serve to bring out, not only their comparative importance, but also relations between one or more of them which were not apparent or could not have been apparent at the time the text was first read. The original sentences or descriptions will then be found sometimes inadequate, and a new phrase will have to be devised that fits a group of references that can be brought together.

The grouping into a number of subparagraphs needs to be judicious. It may well be convenient to number them and to give them headings, and it is often a useful guide to list the numbered subheadings after the main heading, if the article is a long one, so that the reader knows how far down to look for what he wants. Paragraphs and subparagraphs should not be so long that they become wearisome to skim through if the reader wishes to ascertain all that there is under any particular heading or subheading. In this careful breaking up of the subject matter to show the pattern of its treatment lies the fascination of indexing: the discovering of relations and relativities and putting like to like.

In this process, which might be called that of constructive sorting, it is best to concentrate first on the long and more complex entries. They will set the pattern to which in a more simplified form the shorter articles may easily be fitted. There must over the whole, however, be consistency of tone, even though the overall pattern may allow for variation. If, for instance, the indexer has decided upon alphabetization for the arrangement of the descriptive material under each heading or subheading, he may occasionally drop the alphabetization in shorter paragraphs where the departure from it can be detected at a glance. If, on the other hand, the general plan is to arrange the descriptive material in the order of its appearance in the text, the indexer should not have recourse to the alphabet where it happens to suit him. That is to say, if the basic pattern is complex, it may be varied where appropriate by introducing a more simplified form. If the basic pattern is simple, variation by way of making it more complex may confuse and irritate. It is, however, a question of tone rather than of rule, and in indexing as in any literary effort tone is the effect of the quality of the mind at work upon it.

# 7

# *INDEXING OF PERIODICALS*

PETER FERRIDAY[1]

For Great Britain alone some 5500 periodicals are listed in *The Newspaper Press Directory*, while according to Ayer's (annual) *Directory of Periodicals* there are well over 20,000 published in the United States and Canada.[2] By no means are all provided with indexes, although the great majority ought to have at least an annual index. This is especially true of those periodicals that cover the proceedings of learned societies if they are to be of the slightest use to the researcher.

Now the primary function of an index to a periodical is to indicate the location of a specific item. A complete or analytical search is usually not the intention of the user of such indexes. But there are exceptions where a fairly comprehensive index is required, especially in the cases of periodicals in which an abstract section forms a significant feature, or of periodicals that provide an important source of information in a given subject field.

## Types of Periodicals

The kind of index required will depend on the type of periodical itself—on such factors as its subject and special

[1]The first eleven paragraphs did not occur in Ferriday's original paper. They were added here by the Editor (with the general approval of Ferriday) and, it is hoped, will provide a constructive introduction to the art of indexing periodicals.

[2]These figures are quoted from R. L. Collison's *Indexes and Indexing*, 2d. ed., 1959.

Copyright © 1968 by Peter Ferriday.

features, or on the nature of thought it communicates, as well as its bulk and the type of its user.

On the basis of their features periodicals may be roughly grouped as follows: (1) news journals; (2) fiction magazines, not usually requiring an index; (3) journals of learned societies; (4) periodicals of general science or technology; (5) technical and trade journals; and (6) abstracts and review periodicals.

## Features Peculiar to Periodical Indexes

While the general principles of indexing remain constant, there are several aspects of periodicals and newspapers which call for special attention. In the first place, the indexing of periodicals is usually spread over a period of time, normally of one year in the case of journals and magazines; but a daily newspaper may need a quarterly or even bi-monthly index. Again, where the periodical's pagination starts afresh with each issue—and this is invariably the practice with newspapers—it is essential in indexing any item to give not only the page reference but also the number of the issue or its identifying month or date.

Unlike the average book, the periodical will contain a number of independent articles, often dealing with widely divergent topics and always by many different authors. The greatest care must be taken in the selection of standard subject headings in order to insure uniformity not only as between the various installments being indexed but for future installments as well. Once chosen, a subject heading must be rigidly adhered to, cross references being used from synonyms when necessary. But here a word of caution is needed. It sometimes happens that in the course of time verbal usage alters. For instance, the disease that was once commonly known as infantile paralysis is now almost invariably referred to by its proper medical term, poliomyelitis. When the adoption of such a new heading becomes necessary, the old one should continue to be inserted in the index (at least for a time) with a cross reference to the new.

To what extent should the subjects contained in periodical articles be indexed? Numerous periodical indexes are limited to little more than one subject heading per article. But this is rarely enough. Many an article will contain, in addition to its general subject, valuable information on other topics that may be subsequently sought for and which surely deserve their own headings. All that can here be said is that the depth of indexing will have to depend on the type of periodical, the class and range of its readership, and above all on the amount of space the editor or publisher is prepared to allow for the index.

A number of periodicals have separate indexes for "Authors" and "Subjects," but to this writer the practice seems pointless. H. B. Wheatley spent years of his life campaigning for "the index, one and indivisible." After all, an author may himself be also a subject and it is annoying to have to consult more than one index in order to find all the information available about him.

Where classified headings are employed, such as "Obituary" or "Reviews," each subject forming a subheading must also be given its own heading in the index. In the case of "Reviews" it is suggested that the most convenient method is to arrange the subheadings according to the works' titles and the individual headings under the names of their authors.

## The Indexing of Newspapers

Newspaper indexing presents its own particular problems. *The Times* (London), which is one of the very few papers to *publish* its own index over a period, employs a staff of seven to compile this, bi-monthly. Time is the chief factor here. Each of its more experienced indexers is expected to scan—not read—about 45,000 words for indexable news value, and write probably 500 references under relevant headings, *in one day*.

On the choice of subject headings let me quote Mr. C. H. J. Kyte,[3] the editor of *The Times Index*:

> Although some subjects are collected under a general heading, we try where possible to put subjects to a particular title. This is where we differ from the *New York Times Index*. I have an example of how the same story is treated by us and by the *New York Times Index*. It is about the plan to replace London Bridge. In the *Index to The Times* it is under *London Bridge—rebuilding plans*, with no cross-references. In the *New York Times Index* it is under *Bridges*, with the subheading *Thames River Crossing*, and then there is a run-on giving a précis of the news-story.
>
> Another example is their treatment of the Los Angeles race riots last year. In the *Index to The Times* it is under *United States: Negroes: California—Los Angeles riots*, with a cross-reference from Los Angeles. In the *New York Times Index* all the references to Negroes are collected, but there are so many that they have been broken up into sections and numbered. The cross-reference reads: *Los Angeles see Negroes* 129, 131, 146, 150, 162, 168, 179, 187 (for Watts riots).

## The Examination of Indexes

Considering how much periodicals differ in scope, size, and frequency of appearance, it would be absurd to suggest that there could be but one method of compilation of their indexes that would be suitable to them all. The most convenient way of discussing the subject and of avoiding largely irrelevant generalities is by examining some current indexes[4] with the idea of determining how effective they are and how they might be improved. Even here there is a danger; it is very easy to pick on faults and omissions and so give the impression of total inadequacy when in fact the user of the index might be satisfied ninety times out of a hundred. Similarly it has to be remembered that thorough indexing

[3] Kyte, C. H. J., "*The Times* Index," *The Indexer*, Vol. V, No. 3 (Spring, 1967), p. 127.

[4] Not all the examples quoted are from recent issues and the form of some of the indexes may have changed. [Editor]

must be expensive and the perfunctoriness of many indexes may just as well derive from economies as from failures on the indexer's part.

## Early Indexes

The need for indexes has been realized as long as there have been periodicals, and it is useful to note how two early indexes were compiled, partly because they are of some interest in themselves and partly because they bear on current practice.

In 1821 the *Gentleman's Magazine* published an extensive two-volume index for the years 1787–1818. Still of great value, it has its limitations. What these are can best be illustrated by quoting a sequence of entries, omitting volume and page numbers:

> Lort, Rev. Dr. Michael, character of his writings
> Lort, Roger, monument at Tenby
>     [no reference or entry at Tenby]
> Lothesley, manor, tenure of
> Lothian, John Kerr, Marquis of
>     [no reference from Kerr]
> Lothingland, Island, account of
> Lotos, the plant deified
> Lotteries
> Lotus. See Lotos
> Lovat, Rev. John Salt
> Love's Labour Lost
>     [series of entries followed by "See Shakespeare"]

From this it can easily be seen that if you look for single names and place names you are likely to be rewarded; if you want material on a more extensive subject, then the index is of little value. It lacks the necessary references and, relying almost entirely upon one word in the title of the article, is to a large extent accidental in its arrangement The index to the first twelve volumes of *Notes and Queries*, published in 1856, is similar. One sequence runs:

> Jennens, or Jennings, of Acton Place, Suffolk
>     [no reference from Acton Place]
> Jennings Family of Shropshire

    Jerdan (Wm.), his testimonial
    Jeroboam of claret
        [no entry under claret]
    Jersey, gold chair found in
        [entry under "Chair of gold found at . . ."]
    Jersey muse
    Jesse (E.), notes on his "London"
        [no reference under London]

Here the need for double entry has been recognized, but there is a complete want of consistency as well as some ill-considered choice of the key word under which to index: Who would look under "Jeroboam" for an article on claret? The method is a simple one, that of selecting the key word in the title and reversing the order so that it stands first, but a dangerous one since it depends on the essential subject word being in the title. On how many occasions this did not happen could be determined only by elaborate checking.

## Modern Examples

With these examples of pioneering indexes in mind it is interesting to turn to a selection of current indexes. One would expect great changes and improvements. A brief examination of recent indexes shows a surprising uncertainty of principle in compilation, and behind that, perhaps, an uncertainty as to what is required of the index by the user.

*Public Administration* is a quarterly journal. Its separate annual index is in three parts. The articles are listed in the order they appeared, quarter by quarter, in part one. Part two is a list of books reviewed, arranged alphabetically. Part three is a list of authors. In all parts reference is to page number, but there is a preliminary note on the pagination of the quarters. This form of index seems almost valueless. If one has the periodical then it would be as quick, or nearly so, to skim the contents lists of the parts, and it is hardly conceivable that anybody would take the index separately. A similar objection applies to the index of the *Church Quarterly Review*, although its arrangement is different. Here the index, in two parts, lists entirely by author: first, the articles under their authors' names alphabetically; and second, the books reviewed arranged under their authors' names. Reference is made to the first page but there is no key to which part the page appeared in. The index to *Adult Education* consists of one alphabetical sequence of titles and authors and would save little time over scanning the contents lists of the parts. Generally it seems that annual indexes to the ordinary run of quarterly periodicals are not worth producing; they seem to be issued from force of habit.

*The Burlington Magazine* is one of the world's scholarly journals, and that in a field in which the greatest accuracy is necessary. It is not surprising that its index is elaborate. It is divided into six parts: first, a contents list month by month; second, artists and craftsmen, alphabetically arranged and giving details of works referred to; third, authors with the titles of their contributions; fourth, ownership, public—by name of institution; fifth, ownership, private—by personal name; sixth, book reviews in a classified arrangement. This appears to be admirable until one looks carefully and discovers that the main section—artists and craftsmen—refers in its page numbers to illustrations only. Thus there is no *subject* section at all. Since most of the articles are illustrated, the disadvantage is not so great as it might seem at first. Where there are a number of Poussin illustrations one can assume an article round about those pages. But if there had been a letter or a correction to the article in the next issue, it would not appear in conjunction with the original unless it were illustrated. The only way of checking is to work through the author list. This basic deficiency in not providing a complete *subject* section is inexplicable in such a detailed index.

*The Listener's* six-monthly index is fairly elaborate. It is a one-sequence alphabetical index including authors' names and subjects, usually by inverted or straightforward title. No other information is given: that is, the author's name appears without the title of his contribution and vice versa.

For titles there is a considerable amount of double entering in order to give a semblance of subject indexing. "Roe deer in East Anglia" appears also under "Deer," but not under "East Anglia." But "Some problems of coronary heart disease" appears only under "Coronary" and not under "Heart" or "Disease." This compromise of partial double entry and no subject references must be found wanting. There is an attempt, again by double entering, to collect items under such main headings as "Africa," "Architecture," "Art," "Birds," "Communism," "Education," "France," "Gardening," and so forth. But for all its deficiences this index is a useful one.

The index to *Discovery* is a curious combination of method. The first part is an alphabetical list of articles by title, the second part a list of books reviewed, by title, and the third part a subject index to contents, providing a subject heading and page reference. Its form is a compromise between the actual wording of the title of the article and the subject heading pure and simple. Consequently we get some curious subjects: "World food shortage"; "World oil consumption"; "World population problem." These references also appear under "Food," "Oil," and "Population." But as a compromise between title-word and subject indexing— a compromise which is bound to have serious disadvantages—the index must be counted among the better ones.

The index of volumes 31 to 50 of *The Modern Language Review*, running to 216 pages, has a seventy-page subject section. This provides a lengthy example of the confusion of title-word and subject indexing. "Ibsen, the proverb in" does not appear under "Proverbs." "Songs, Old French" has no reference from "French songs," nor "Snobbery, three satirists of" from "Satire." Most curiously, considering that it is an entirely literary magazine, the largest section is under "Literature," divided by French, German, and so forth. And yet there are no references from "French literature" to "Literature, French," and so on. There are all sorts of confusions, for example, "Romanticism, *See under* Literature." Obviously very little preliminary thought was given to the principle of arrangement; it oscillates between subject, broad classification, and title-word arrangement. It seems extraordinary that when such a large index was being considered so little serious planning was given to it.

The index to a recent volume of a British scientific journal is distressing.[5] It is a single alphabetical sequence index of authors, titles, and subjects derived from title words. The results, because of the manic thoroughness, are delightful. Sir John Hammond reviewed a book by Dr. Allan Fraser called *Animal Husbandry Heresies* and the review was titled "Animal Husbandry." This gives rise in the index to the following entries:

> Animal Husbandry, *reviewed* by Sir John Hammond, 47
> Animal Husbandry Heresies (Dr. Allan Fraser), *review* by Sir John Hammond, 47
> Husbandry: Animal, *review* by Sir John Hammond, 47
> Husbandry (Animal) Heresies (Dr. Allan Fraser), *review* by Sir John Hammond, 47
> Heresies: Animal Husbandry (Dr. Allan Fraser), *review* by Sir John Hammond, 47
> Fraser, Dr. Allan: Animal Husbandry Heresies, *review* by Sir John Hammond, 47
> Hammond, Sir John: Animal Husbandry, *review*, 47

Seven entries for one review! This is not at all exceptional. For an article called "Seasonal Variation of the Sea Surface Temperature in Coastal Waters of the British Isles" by F. E. Lumb, published for the Meteorological Office, Air Ministry, there are eleven entries, under "Seasonal," "Variation," "Sea," "Surface," "Temperature," "Coastal," "Waters," "British," "Lumb," "Air Ministry," "Meteorological Office." The inversions and convolutions of the title are marvelous and masterpieces of typography. An article called "Influence of Large Doses of Oestrogens on the Structure of the Bones of some Reptiles" appears as follows:

> Bones of some Reptiles: Influence of Large Doses of Oestrogens on the Structure of the

[5]This was written in 1963. The journal has now a new indexer, and new methods are employed. [Editor]

Doses (Large), of Oestrogens: Influence of, on the Structure of the
Bones of some Reptiles

Influence of Large Doses of Oestrogens on the Structure of the
Bones of some Reptiles

Large Doses of Oestrogens: Influence of, on the Structure of the
Bones of some Reptiles

Oestrogens: Influence of Large Doses of, on the Structure of the
Bones of some Reptiles

Reptiles: Influence of Large Doses of Oestrogens on the Structure
of the Bones of some

Structure of the Bones of some Reptiles: Influence of Large Doses
of Oestrogens on the

Added to these seven entries there is an author entry. The procedure is on the face of it absurd, quite apart from the cost of setting and proofreading. Idiocies abound. If Britain, as against Great Britain, appears in the title it comes under "Britain" only. "University of Birmingham" has no reference from "Birmingham University." The whole method leads to the index for one quarter taking up 107 double-column pages.

The system of subject indexing by title words can be absurdly wasteful and quite ineffective. In a scientific journal one is not likely to go far wrong because the titles are very brief abstracts. But in other sorts of journals there can be curious results. A year or two ago *The Economist* ingeniously entitled an article "The Old Lady Shows her Amber." This would go under "Old," "Lady," and "Amber" on the pattern referred to earlier. But Amber was a reference to traffic lights; Old Lady, to her of Threadneedle Street; and the subject was the raising of the bank rate.

That earlier index may have been misconceived, but the one to the *Journal* of the Royal Society of Arts has faults which render it all but valueless. A series of lectures on photography in education, industry and commerce, and medicine is not indexed under education, industry, commerce, or medicine. A lecture on Restoration portraits does not appear under portraits; a notice of the Peter Floud Memorial Prize does not appear under Floud; a lecture on economic developments in Canada does not appear under

Canada. In short the whole basis of the index is to accept only the first key word as the point of entry, expecting the user to remember the title of the article he is looking for. Inevitably one comes to doubt if the index fills any real function at all. To be set against this is the index to the photographic periodical, *Perspective*, with its entirely satisfactory arrangement of title and collection of key words to produce subject indexing. The arrangement has been devised by someone who evidently gave thought to the purpose of an index and who did not assume that the searcher already knows the title of the article he wants.

## Title or Subject?

Reference to the development of indexes of groups of periodicals may be useful in considering ways in which indexes to particular periodicals might develop. *Poole's Index to Periodical Literature* covering the years 1802–1881 and published in 1882 was constructed on the usual index pattern, relying on key words brought to the front by changing the order of the title. The method led to the familiar faults and these were increased by the fact that the index was the product of many hands: an article on "Drainage of Calcutta" appeared under "Calcutta" without a reference under "Drainage," though there was an article on "Drainage of London" under "Drainage," but without any appearance under "London." Reform was at that time in progress through the publication of Cutter's *Rules for a Dictionary Catalog* in 1876, and what was taught there bore fruit in *The Readers' Guide to Periodical Literature*, 1901. Here was a one-sequence subject and author index with a consistent set of subject headings and a thorough and regular form of references. There was no dependence on the change of key words appearing in the title of articles. For the first time real order was offered, not merely verbal jiggery-pokery. Such indexes have gone on developing right down to the *British Technology Index* where the subject headings are as specific as possible, and its techniques therefore more relevant to the problems of indexing single periodicals.

There are obvious differences between the two forms of index, but clearly such a method as that employed in the *British Technology Index* relates closely to any form of periodical indexing. By comparison most of the indexes examined are of the pre-Cutter era. The "Standards for Indexes to Learned and Scientific Periodicals" published in *The Indexer* suggested some minimum requirements: "Articles in journals should be indexed under the authors, titles, significant words in titles, and under the subject dealt with in the text. Some articles may require many entries for subjects, synonyms and for authorities quoted." Had this been accepted most of the faults cited would have been avoided, but it is noticeable how persistent even now the significant-words-in-titles idea is; here it is even more curious since subject indexing is insisted upon. It surely seems time that the principle of subject indexing without reference to the author's or the editor's choice of words for the title were adopted. One feels, too, some doubt about the need in many cases for a title entry. Obviously if the index is to be an expensively produced one, the title should be included; but it would be interesting to know how often the title of a magazine article is accurately remembered. The inclusion of titles seems to be based on the idea, a dubious one, that the titles of novels and of periodical articles are analogous. One can imagine an inquirer, of no exceptional memory, looking up *Anna Karenina* or *The Mill on the Floss* but hardly "Spark-advance device for electronic ignition" or "Why change to decimals?" (With reference to this it is interesting to note that the former article appears in the *British Technology Index* under words not given in the title, "Petrol," "Engines," "Ignition," "Spark-advance units." There were also the necessary "*See* references" from "Spark-advance units," "Ignition," and so on.

Obviously there are complicating features in periodical indexing that have scarcely been touched on in this chapter, but it does seem apparent that much current indexing is unsatisfactory in method and application. Indexes seem at present constructed for those who know what they are looking for, to the extent of the word order of titles, and therefore are not likely to use the index at all. But the majority of users must surely wish to use an index in order to locate an article *about* something or *by* somebody. The author entry is a straightforward matter; the problem lies with the subject entry, and the examples given may have displayed the deficiencies of many indexes in that respect. The development required would seem to be in the direction of subject indexing as used in the *British Technology Index* or *Perspective* and the abandonment of the hazard involved in using such notions as "significant words" and "key words from the titles."

# 8

# *SCIENTIFIC AND TECHNICAL INDEXING, I*

J. EDWIN HOLMSTROM

This chapter will begin with a few fundamental remarks on indexing in general and lead up to an explanation of how the indexing of scientific and technical material differs from that of other material. The first part will be devoted to stating the basic principles, and the final part to discussion and advice on the mechanics to be adopted for making an index in accordance with them.

## The Objects of Indexing

As regards the objects it is meant to serve, indexing can be broadly defined as including any device helpful for discovering or rediscovering in a book or in a collection of papers or notes, such items of information or passages of text as have a wanted relevance. [See also DEFINITIONS, p. 10, Editor.] Here the stress is on the words "discovering *or rediscovering*," because an index should be able to supply answers to either or both of the following two questions:

> I am interested in a certain topic: Does this volume contain information that might be useful to me in thinking or acting on it?
> I have reason to believe this volume contains a reference or references to a certain topic which interests me: At what page numbers are they?

Note that these are two separate questions, although interrelated. The first can be answered without the need for an index in the ordinary sense appended to the book, if an adequate list of contents is provided at the beginning. (By "adequate" is meant that the list of contents must not be limited to the chapter headings alone but must include under each chapter head a list of the sections into which it is divided, or else a few lines summarizing what the chapter as a whole contains. An amplified contents list of this kind is easier, quicker, and cheaper to prepare than the sort of index this chapter is about). This fact is worth bearing in mind from the point of view of what might be called the principle of overall economy, which applies equally to book indexing and to the filing and indexing of business or administrative papers. It can be stated as follows: every item which someone conceivably might want must be made findable without fail; but it is not necessary and would be bad economics (a wasteful use of scarce resources) to make all the items findable with equal ease. If a particular item is certain or very likely to be wanted, those who want it should be enabled to find it instantly; but if it is unlikely to be wanted except by a very few, it is more economical to oblige those few to spend some time and effort in the search—as long as they are sure of finding it ultimately—than to pay for extra time and effort, paper and printing, in making the index more complete. The criterion for maximum *overall* economy is that over a period of years the total expenditure of effort, time, and money by whoever pays for the index, plus the aggregate expenditure of time and effort by everyone who uses the index, should be a minimum. Let us not labor this point unduly, but it is important and, though obvious, often overlooked.

An index, then, is a device for discovering or rediscovering items that have a wanted relevance. This latter may mean either something associated with a particular name (a personal or place name, the name of a company or organization, a trade name, etc.), or something related to a particular subject field or topic of discussion.

Names are much easier to index than subject designations: all the indexer has to do is to put them in alphabetical order, which in ninety-nine cases out of a hundred raises no sort of difficulty or ambiguity to either the indexer or the user of the index. In the hundredth case, such as that of a surname beginning with Mc or preceded by de or De or von, a name transliterated from a non-Latin script, a geographical name whose original form differs from that used in English, certain rules need to be applied. [See those in Chapters 3 and 4, pp. 40–41, 47–48, and 64–65—Editor] Opinion is divided over whether a book should have a name index (or perhaps a personal names index and also a geographical index) separate from its subject index. [See Chapters 5 and 6.] American practice tends to favor putting everything together in what librarians call a "dictionary catalogue," but some British publishers prefer to have the name index separate.

## Subject Indexes

A subject index is essentially an ordered arrangement of symbols, each of which stands for a different thing or a different concept. The two essentials are: first, that the symbols chosen to represent potentially interesting features mentioned in the text of the book should be distinctive and mutually exclusive (each symbol being associated in everybody's mind with only one idea or thing); and second, that they should be capable of being arranged in some easily perceptible sequence or pattern whereby any wanted symbol can readily be located in the index—each symbol being followed by the number of the page where the wanted information is to be found. Fundamentally there are two principles on which a pattern of such symbols can be laid out.

One method is to use numbers, like those scheduled in the Universal Decimal Classification, or mixtures of letters and numbers like those adopted in certain library classifications, each group of which serves as a label for the pigeonholing of references to particular concepts and each of which is related to the other symbols according to a systematic or hierarchical conceptual scheme. In other words these symbols indicate the positions of concepts in a map of knowledge. Given this, one can find his way from one idea to another rather as he finds his way from one place to another with the aid of a geographical map. (Sometimes one needs also an alphabetical key index to the classification, in order to discover the coordinates of wanted features in the map of knowledge if he knows only their designations, just as one needs an alphabetical gazetteer appended to an atlas in order to find places when he knows only their names.) This is the principle commonly preferred for the library *cataloguing* of whole books, the books being classified under symbols according to their main subjects. Using bastard Greek words one could call the cataloguing and the arranging of books, treating each whole book as a unit, "macro-indexing" to distinguish it from the "micro-indexing" of the detailed contents within each book. Incidentally it is interesting, though perhaps not very realistic at present, to speculate about whether the micro-indexing of books and the macro-indexing of their contents may some day be standardized and merged into one single system embodied in some vast central computer.

The alternative principle whereby to arrange indicative symbols of information relevance, is that known as alphabetical indexing. When one thinks of it, this is really a rather odd sort of classification. It classifies concepts not according to their actual nature and their logical inter-relationships, but according to the different sounds which people utter when they talk about the different concepts or imagine when they think about them. It has some practical disadvantages, too. Alphabetical indexing is not suitable for international use because individuals who have grown up in different countries associate different sounds with the same concepts (or with what they sometimes wrongly believe to be the same concepts). Moreover even within a single language area, and even in science, the terminology in current use is very far from being standardized, and the technical terms currently employed are not in fact the tools of precision for pinpointing and distinguishing the various concepts which they ideally ought to be. Hence there is much confusion and a blurring of the significance attached to the words that are used in communication and, incidentally, in alphabetical indexing. Such ambiguities occur, among other reasons, because of the existence of homonyms (cases where the same word is used with more than one meaning according to the context), synonyms (cases where two or more words are in use to mean the same thing), or what is worse, quasi-synonyms (where several different words mean approximately but not quite the same things, so that there is a blurring of the edges of their meanings). In some fields even the differences between American and British terminology are apt to cause confusion.

Odd as its principle may be and despite the need for precautions and circumspection in using it, the writer is of the opinion that alphabetical indexing will nevertheless continue generally to be preferred over systematic classification as a means of locating wanted relevances within individual books and within completed volumes of periodicals. The rest of this chapter will be based on this assumption. The great advantage of alphabetical indexing, which is found to outweigh its disadvantages, lies in the fact that anybody who knows the alphabet can use an alphabetical index without any need for instruction or explanation.

## Characteristics of Scientific Indexes

Now, as regards scientific books, are there indeed any respects in which these need to be indexed differently from other literature? The writer would suggest that there are certain quite marked differences which derive from the very nature of science and from the preconditions for scientific progress. It is important to appreciate this, and the next few paragraphs will be devoted to it.

Science is organized knowledge. The aim pursued by "pure" scientists is the clarification and amplification of our understanding of phenomena. This is accomplished by arranging observed and recorded facts in patterns and by trying to discern recurrent relationships in those patterns. When these scientists have discovered a relationship that goes on recurring, they call it a hypothesis and they test it by experiment; if the experiment is found to confirm the hypothesis, both qualitatively and quantitatively, however many times it is repeated, then this discovery is put forward as a scientific law. What "applied" scientists do is to look for ways of turning the world's accumulated knowledge of such laws to human advantage in the various fields of technology, engineering, medicine, agriculture, and so on. Thus science, both pure and applied, depends for its advancement upon an interplay continually taking place between purposefully directed experimental research and efficiently exploited records of what has already been ascertained. These two, research and records, are complementary necessities. They alternate with one another. Somebody achieves an advance in knowledge; its application gives rise to new problems that are then investigated in their turn, and the results of the investigation add a further flow into the stream of documentation, which is to science what the circulation of blood is to the body.

The point made by this diversion is that the scientist's or the technologist's motive in consulting a scientific or technical book is quite different from the motive that animates the reader of a historical or political or what might generally be called a "literary" book. One reads the latter as an end in itself—for enjoyment, for education, for culture—because he is interested in the theme of that particular book *as a whole*, and perhaps also in the manifestation of its author's personality. A person reading or consulting a scientific book, however, is relatively uninterested in the arrangement or character or authorship of the book as such. What he hopes for is to find data or speculations in it which he can use for his own work, in order to begin, himself, from the level already reached by antecedent workers as recorded in their publications, and to go on from that point to create something newer. He regards scientific books and periodicals (especially those containing the transactions of learned societies and professional bodies) as a sort of quarry from which he can extract data to be combined with the results of his own work in order to raise knowledge of the field to a higher level. These differences in the reasons why literary and scientific people read or consult books, are, and ought to be, reflected in differences in the indexing of works in their respective fields.

## The Varieties of Scientific Publications

The various kinds of scientific publications can be set down as forming a kind of spectrum:

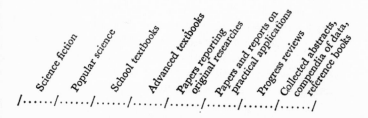

What this should bring out is that the varieties of publications named on the left merge into general literature as regards the reasons why people read them, whereas when one proceeds from left to right the publications in question become more purely "scientific" in the sense just explained. The science fiction and popular science books on the extreme left are followed by school textbooks of a rather more "scientific" character, and then by advanced textbooks such as those intended for undergraduates. With the aid of the latter the student is led up nearer to the frontiers of existing knowledge and is progressively initiated into the techniques employed for exploring beyond those frontiers. The results of such explorations are reported in papers written by research scientists, and the further gains in knowledge that accrue from the application of "pure"

science to practical ends are reported in the writings of the technologists and others concerned. Aids to following these developments in outline are exemplified in the annually published progress reviews covering particular fields such as physics or chemistry, which serve also as frameworks for bibliographical references to the original sources of the data mentioned in them. Finally on the extreme right of the spectrum are the reference books, such as collections of abstracts and compendia of established data like the Beilstein handbook for organic chemistry, the Gmelin handbook for inorganic chemistry, and corresponding works for other fields of science. Such publications contain no "literature" in the ordinary sense of the word; their purpose is to bring together, in an organized form, masses of data and indications of where still more detailed data may be found.

The point made here is that the further one goes to the right the more essential it becomes that the indexing be of a kind that will serve efficiently the scientists' and technologists' peculiar needs. It has to be as detailed and as many-sided as possible, consistently with what was called earlier the principle of maximum overall economy, but weighted in the direction of putting more work on the indexer so as to save work for its user, because an active scientist's time is too precious to the community to justify frittering it away in hunting for elusive references. Indeed, on the extreme right of the spectrum the indexes become as important as the textual contents of the book and may need to occupy a comparable amount of the total space.

To illustrate: The finest example of the possibilities of alphabetical indexing at the extreme right-hand end of the spectrum is the American journal *Chemical Abstracts*. This is what is sometimes called a secondary publication because its object is to supply, not the information itself in full, but awareness of where the information is to be found in the primary publications, with just enough summary for the reader to be able to decide whether it will be worth his while to consult the original sources. Chemistry is an especially difficult field to cover in this way because of the extent and complication of its special terminology and nomenclature. *Chemical Abstracts* appears fortnightly, and at the end of the year it contains synopses of about 70,000 articles that have appeared in some 5,500 primary journals published all over the world, as well as of about 12,000 chemical patents in eighteen countries. The indexes published on completion of each annual volume contain as many as 650 words for every 1,000 words of the text. In 1952 (but they may be bigger still now) they comprised a subject index of 1,586 pages, an "empirical formula" index of 347 pages, and a patent index (by patentees' names and countries) of 16 pages. The cumulated decennial index from 1937 to 1946 had about two million entries.

## Differences from "Literary" Indexes

Apart from thoroughness, the most prominent differences between a good index to a scientific book and a good index to a literary work are perhaps the following two.

Scientific advance is an integrative process. Each contributor to it assumes an obligation to mention the antecedent contributors so that every statement can be verified and amplified by tracing it back to its origins. For this purpose every scientific publication mentions a multitude of bibliographical references, preferably not in footnotes but brought together in a list at the end of each chapter (or sometimes at the end of the book as a whole), and cited in the text either by serial numbers or by authors' names. So much importance is attached to these citations that it is common practice to make the names index or author index of the book indicate not only the page numbers where each of the antecedent authors is mentioned in the text, but also the page numbers at which the bibliographical references are given with all the necessary detail for tracing them in libraries. (The latter numbers can be distinguished from the former by putting them in italics. This is useful because in a string of perhaps twenty or thirty page numbers after some exceptionally prolific author's name, the page numbers printed in italics will be those at the ends of the chapters, and the reader can tell from the list of contents of the book the most likely subject relevance of the citations in the text which have the intermediate page numbers.)

The second important difference in the indexing compared with that of a literary work lies in the manner and extent to which a multiplicity of index entries that are some way interrelated may or may not be grouped together under a main heading. Take for instance the excellent index to A. P. J. Taylor's *English History 1914–1945.* Under the main heading "British Expeditionary Force 1939" one finds the following sequence of subheadings printed in run-on form:

> Promised, 436; sent to France, 459; on Belgian frontier, 460; advances into Belgium, 484/485; evacuated from Dunkirk, 486; losses of, 487; . . . .

In a narrative work this is probably as good an arrangement as any, because more often than not the sequence of the page numbers will correspond approximately to the sequence of the events recorded or to the time sequence in which the questions discussed were raised. But in a scientific book this kind of sequence would be unsuitable, because the user of such books is not primarily interested in the stages through which science has developed; what he wants is the results and data which the earlier development has yielded so that he himself can build on these in his own work. The index, therefore, is more efficient if the subheadings under any given main heading are printed on separate lines (not in the form of a paragraph), arranged in the alphabetical order of the words with which they begin, as in the following example:

> Dipole
>   characteristic impedance of
>     circular cross section, 109
>     multiwire cage, 113
>     square cross section, 112
>     triangular cross section, 112
>   definition of, 55
>   effect of shape near drive point, 108
>   electric, 55, 66

In this example the subheading "characteristic impedance of" is further split into four sub-subheadings. This is a fairly common practice, but most publishers do not like to go beyond the third stage of subdivision; and rightly so, because overindulgence in subdividing confuses alphabetical indexing with systematic classification. As remarked at the beginning of this chapter, these are two different principles and they do not mix well. If what ought to be a straight alphabetical sequence of terms denoting different things is interrupted by pockets of attempted systematic classifications of the things themselves—"concealed classifications" as they have aptly been called—the only effect is to bewilder the user of the index by leaving him in doubt as to where he ought to look for what he wants.

## The Entries

The writer sees no objection to the key word being sometimes an adjective or an adverb,[1] if this assists the user of the index in finding references to the particularity that interests him. What matters is that each main heading and subheading should begin with as concrete and expressive a word as possible so as to catch the searcher's eye and characterize exactly the items he may be looking for. On this principle, for instance, "Portal frames wind resistance designing formulae" is a better index entry than one beginning with the word "formulae". "Test results table" is preferable to "Table of test results," and "Ship design computer programs library" is more suitable than "Library of computer programs for ship design."

[1] In some indexes, adjectives (including participles) as key words are almost as common as nouns. Adverbs are far less frequent; a striking and effective instance of one occurs in Holmstrom's own index to *The Sea* (John Wiley & Sons, 1962):

Aerodynamically:
  rough flow, 81
  smooth flow, 80

The use of prepositions as key words, e.g., "Without body murders" (an actual example from a recent index) should be avoided, except when the preposition forms part of a title, e.g., "In the interests of the Brethren" (Kipling). [Editor]

In all alphabetical indexing it is perpetually a moot point whether to enter any given item as a subheading under a main heading that denotes a more general concept or to make it an independent main heading in its own right. A similar question is whether to invert entries. To give a simple example: Should "Lead pipes" be changed to "Pipes, lead"? Someone studying the different uses of lead would be better served by the former; someone studying hydraulics perhaps better by the latter. It can be argued that "Electron microscope" should be inverted so as to bring the entries "Microscope, electron" and "Microscope, optical" together in the index, but that as "Mass spectrograph" is based on a different principle and serves a different purpose from an ordinary spectrograph it is thought of as beginning with "m" and so ought not to be inverted. These questions are debatable, and it is difficult to lay down any definitive rule, with due regard to economy in indexing. In many cases it may be considered worth while to repeat the entries both ways.

In the writer's opinion it is generally better, when in doubt, to make each index entry a separate main heading rather than to subordinate it to another, unless either (a) it begins with the same word or words as another entry, in which case it may be convenient to group them together, or (b) the entry by itself does not make sense or would be ambiguous unless read in the context defined by a main heading. The second of these cases is important where the same word carries different meanings according to the context. This often happens in engineering; for instance, "Condenser (steam)" is quite a different thing from "Condenser (electrical)."

## The "Mechanics"

Now let us consider the actual working procedures that can be adopted for preparing the indexes to a scientific book.

The first step is to agree with the publisher approximately how big and detailed the index is to be. Obviously it would be satisfying to try to make an absolutely complete and logically perfect index, one in which the user could be quite certain of locating quickly whatever he wanted—every conceivable synonym and quasi-synonym being mentioned with a cross reference to the entry word actually adopted. In practice, however, this ideal is ruled out by economics, and realistically speaking the problem becomes one of making as perfect an index as possible within the limits set by cost, time, and space.

So far as the writer knows, no systematic research has been published comparing the densities of indexing desirable in scientific books. It varies with the subject and nature of the book, but an average of between two and three index entries per page of text seems to be usual.

Other questions that are best settled before starting work on an index include whether the alphabetization is to be word-by-word or letter-by-letter, whether commas or some other punctuation signs are to be used, whether the final as well as the initial page numbers of items that extend over several pages are to be given (or alternatively the initial page number followed by "ff.," meaning that the same topic occurs on either or both of the next two following pages of text), and whether subheadings as well as main headings are to begin with a capital letter. (The writer is against using capitals unnecessarily; they only make the proper and geographical names less easy to pick out.)

As a kind of "motion study," the actual work of indexing after these details have been settled can be divided into four phases:

1. Becoming acquainted with the book as a whole—its scope and arrangement, its author's objectives in writing it, the proportions of space he has devoted to its various contents, and which of the topics discussed and data presented he evidently considers to be the most important.
2. On this basis, deciding and marking what items are to be indexed. As regards names this raises no problem,

but as regards subjects it calls for a high degree of technically informed judgment. To assert that the indexer needs to be a professionally experienced specialist in the particular subject of each book would be a counsel of perfection; but—like a technical translator—he does need to have an appropriate scientific or technological background combined with common sense, access to reference books, and conscientiousness in never resorting to guesswork.

3. Writing out or preferably typewriting the index entries decided upon and arranging them in alphabetical order as copy for sending to the printer.

4. Checking and later proof reading.

Phase 1 is accomplished by reading the book rapidly. At this stage it is not necessary to concentrate on and ponder over every sentence or even over every paragraph, but it is well to pause at the end of each chapter and mentally summarize what seems to be its gist, using the list of contents as a framework for doing so.

Phase 2 can be carried out in the following way. Read the book again, chapter by chapter, underlining first of all the names and making a tick in the left margin opposite each one of them. Then read each chapter a third time, more carefully. Besides marking any names or ideas that may have been overlooked before, now mark in a different color of ink (a ball-point pen is the ideal instrument for this) the words that appear to be suitable for use as subject index headings. Sometimes a word or short sequence of words appearing in the text will serve for an index heading as it stands, in which case merely underline it and put a tick against it in the right-hand margin. Often, however, words for use as index headings have to be selected or combined differently from the sequence in which they appear in the text, or need to have others added by hand. If so, write little ringed numbers over them and repeat these in the right-hand margin as in the following example:[2]

[2]Taken from *Eddy Currents*, 1967 (see Acknowledgments, p. 8).

7·3.　RESISTANCE OF A LITZ WIRE

In order to reduce skin effect, particularly at higher frequencies, stranding of conductors is used. This is useful also from the viewpoint of flexibility. Individual wires of the strand are enamelled and twisted along the entire divided conductor

Resistance
　Litz wire, 98–102

Litz wire
　resistance, 98–102

Skin effect
　reduced by stranding of conductors, 98

Stranding of conductors, 98

The advantage of this system is that the indexer himself has a minimum of writing and no typing to do. Once he has read and marked the text as just described, the remaining operations can be performed by an assistant with no technical knowledge but able to do accurate copy typing which the indexer can check, item by item, very easily. This is important because indexing is not well paid, and if the clerical part of the job can be done by someone else at a fair clerical rate of payment the indexer's own rate per hour will be more reasonable.

[Another practice is to underline the main headings as follows: *Resistance of Litz wire, 98–102* and *Skin effect reduced by stranding conductors, 98,* and then in the final editing to make the other cards.]

Still another procedure is in three steps: (1) the specialist merely underlines words and phrases; (2) a special indexer makes cards from these underlinings *and* edits them; and (3) a typist makes final copy for printer.

The writer has tried various methods for Phase 3, but as he is still undecided which is best, he will refer to several.

The first he believes is what most indexers use. It consists in writing each index entry on a separate slip of paper or small card and filing these in alphabetical order. [See also Chapter 3.] Typing them instead of writing by hand is very time-consuming: each slip or card must be fed into the machine and taken out again after typing only a few words. If, however, after arranging the cards in alphabetical order the handwritten entries are recopied by typewriter, an additional checking operation becomes necessary to safeguard against typographical errors, which may make the whole job uneconomic. It is true that if the indexer's handwriting (or that of his assistant) is sufficiently disciplined, the printer may sometimes be persuaded to set in type directly from the handwritten slips; but he may charge more for doing so. Separate cards or slips are more troublesome for the compositor than copy supplied in continuous list form. Another and serious objection to separate slips is the amount of time spent in fumbling among those already filed in order to insert a new one in its proper alphabetical position. The waste of time can be reduced, but not eliminated, by having guide cards with projecting tabs marked a, abl, abs, ace, acr, . . . , etc.; but these in turn involve additional work.

For these reasons the writer went over to the "shingled sheets" method, using lined foolscap or quarto paper.

To prepare such sheets, first estimate the approximate total number of entry lines the index will ultimately contain and take enough sheets to accommodate three or four times as many entries. (Do not be afraid of wasting paper.) Count out the sheets into batches of ten. Shingle the bottom edges of the sheets in each batch so that each sheet projects about a quarter inch below the previous sheet and bind each batch of ten shingled sheets with wire staples through the left-hand margin. Mark suitable initial letter groups in the bottom right corners of the shingled sheets to correspond with the proportions in which different parts of the alphabet tend to be occupied in an index. (This can be done by copying the successive initial letter groups from the successive pages in an existing index of roughly the same size, or by copying them from every $n$th page of a technical dictionary, $n$ being chosen to give the right proportion.)

The shingled sheets can then be used for writing the index entries on them directly in what should be the right alphabetical order. But in practice, however much foresight has been used in spreading out the entries alphabetically within each sheet, leaving vacant spaces between them, it will eventually happen that two successive lines are already occupied and a new entry ought to be inserted between them. To provide for this contingency, use only the right half of the sheets at first, so that additions can be made in the left half opposite the points at which they need to be interpolated among those already written on the right.

A practical snag, when using shingled sheets in this way to make a large index, is that their bottom right corners are apt to curl up through much fingering. It may be preferable, therefore, to use a book (or a series of several school exercise books) instead, with the initial letter groups marked on tabs attached one below the other on the edges of the successive sheets in the book.

Whether the sheets are shingled and stapled or are bound in a book, they must necessarily be written upon by hand, and it is difficult to keep them tidy enough for sending to the printer. Unless this is achieved, it means that everything finally has to be copied by typewriter and, therefore, to be rechecked. To avoid this, the writer has lately been experimenting with another method which consists of having the index entries typed direct onto adhesive labels, in the order they happen to come, as illustrated below the example of page marking explained in connection with Phase 2. Self-sticking tacky labels can be typewritten while still attached to the backing sheet of the special paper on which they are sold, after which the backing sheet is torn or cut with scissors into strips, each carrying one label. These are then sorted into heaps on the table in alphabetical order. When this has been done the labels are detached from the strips of backing sheet and stuck onto successive sheets of ordinary paper in individual alphabetical order, one below the other. It is best to start at the end of the index and work upwards from Z to A. Thereby those labels on which a subheading has been typewritten indented under a main heading can be so arranged that the main heading on each label is covered up by the subheading of the label which precedes it in the alphabet, except in the case of the first subheading under any given main heading.

Gummed labels that have to be moistened to make them stick are cheaper than the self-sticking kind. They are sold in rolls with perforations for tearing the successive labels apart after typing, but the tearing operation takes more time than one might expect.

Another method is to used punched cards, which enables the sorting to be done by machine. This would seldom be economic for indexing an ordinary book under ordinary conditions, but the case may be different for a very large one or for a periodical where one is required to produce not only a separate index to each completed volume but later a cumulative index in one alphabetical sequence covering a succession of volumes. Each index entry can be typewritten immediately below the top edge of a card and the latter then punched to correspond with the initial letters (for instance, to represent the first three letters of the first word followed by the first letters of the next following word). When it comes actually to printing the index, the machine sorts them into the correct order, whereupon they are shingled and photocopied to produce copy for the printer.

This procedure, however, is subject to two practical snags: (1) the curvature imparted to the cards by the platen of the typewriter may remain and cause jams when they are passed through the sorter; (2) the shingling operation, by hand, is troublesome and may upset the proper sequence if done inattentively.

Finally it should be mentioned that by an adaptation of any of the procedures here described it is not difficult to prepare an index from galley proofs, before the text has been divided into pages, and add the page numbers later by hand when one can juxtapose the marked galley proofs with page proofs.

# 9

# SCIENTIFIC AND TECHNICAL INDEXING, II

ERIC J. COATES

In case the title of this chapter carries the implication that there is something peculiar or fundamentally different about scientific and technical indexes which marks them off from other kinds of indexing, it should be made clear that the writer does not think so. Very few of the points with which he will deal will have no application to indexing in other subject fields. The main factors that from the indexer's viewpoint distinguish science from nonscience material are questions of degree only. Scientific literature contains a greater number of concepts *in toto* and a far higher proportion of precisely defined concepts than does the literature of the humanities, so that from the point of view of the multiplicity of concepts scientific indexing looks at first glance formidable, but from the point of view of the battle between words and meanings, the scientific indexer gets off relatively lightly. To be sure, despite all essays at standardized nomenclature, there is plenty of ambiguity in scientific, and more particularly technological, terminology. But at least, despite all that is justifiably said about the sheer incompetence of much scientific writing as communication, the scientific author usually does manage to convey the definite topic about which he is writing. The same cannot be said in all fields.

The second difference of degree concerns the consumer side of scientific indexing. Scientific activity has an increasingly serious information problem upon its hands, and a great deal of attention is at the moment being focused upon scientific indexes. Some elaborate experiments have been carried out on the efficiency of such indexes, at Cranfield (Bedfordshire) in Britain, and elsewhere. Taken all in all it would be fair to say that scientific indexes are under particularly close scrutiny, and at the present moment rather more is being expected of them than is the case with other types of indexes.

Some of the interesting things that are being done in connection with scientific indexing are worth considering for the light they throw on the basic purposes and aims of indexing generally. There is the KWIC indexing system, a not too distant variant of which is now being used to provide a current subject approach to chemical literature. KWIC was invented by one of the giant computer-manufacturing concerns seeking to develop fresh uses for computers. It is meant for the indexing of scientific papers, though it is possible to conceive of its use for book indexing. Briefly, the computer is programmed to take each word in the title, with some exceptions to be mentioned shortly, and to print out the title repetitively under each selected word. This is achieved, without disturbing the word order, in this fashion: For the given title "Efficiency and transparency of cheap liquid scintillators" the following is produced:[1]

| | |
|---|---|
| and transparency of | cheap liquid scintillators. efficiency |
| liquid scintillators | efficiency and transparency of cheap |
| transparency of cheap | liquid scintillators. efficiency and |
| of cheap liquid | scintillators. efficiency and transparency |
| efficiency and | transparency of cheap liquid scintillators |

Now you will see that you get an entry under all words in the title except articles, prepositions, and conjunctions. It is of course quite easy to give the computer a list of articles,

---

[1] N.B. The alphabetical arrangement of the index is governed by the first letters after the central space.

prepositions, and conjunctions and instruct it to ignore these; not so easy, and indeed not attempted, is to give it a formula enabling it to reject the valueless entry under CHEAP.[2]

The writer mentions KWIC because it is an outstanding demonstration of indexing at its lowest level of sophistication. All that it requires is that words given in the text (or title, for a bibliographical index) should be picked up and manipulated into alphabetical order. Even at this low level a certain discrimination is needed to reject nonsignificant words, which no one will ever want to look up. We see that the computer can only discriminate to the extent of rejecting a predetermined list of nonsignificant words, and that usually this list comprises only articles, prepositions, and conjunctions. This question of deciding what is or is not significant is the most pervasive unsolved problem of indexing at every level. When we ask ourselves about significance, we should ask "significant to whom?" The significance problem is in inverse proportion to the extent that we can visualize the needs of the person who is going to consult the index, and in general this means that it is an acute problem for an index covering a wide subject field of interest to many different kinds of specialist interest, and less acute for indexes covering narrow subject fields. Even the word CHEAP might be significant in a bibliography or book on "How to sell scientific instruments." We cannot easily overcome the significance problem, which exists in scientific indexing as in other indexing, though we may be able, as in the KWIC system, to whittle it down just a little.

Now let us pass to what can be regarded as indexing of the middle or second degree of sophistication. Before leaving KWIC behind, we should note that for all its wide-open loopholes which will be obvious to all, it is doing a job that at the moment is too big for human indexers or that, what is more important, needs to be done more rapidly than can be carried out by human indexers. It has the virtue of its

[2] Capital letters will be used throughout this chapter in reference to entries.

name. It *is* quick, and speed is of paramount importance in scientific literature indexing. The scientist, particularly the applied scientist, just cannot afford to wait for the leisurely index which comes months or years after the event to which it refers.

The second level of indexing to which we now turn is distinguished from the first in that the indexer is no longer simply a manipulator of words but someone who tries to isolate the concepts signified by the words. His task is to utilize words that will indicate the concepts lying behind the author's words—an unenviable task, and perhaps logically doomed to fall short of 100 per cent success. For this process of signposting the concept behind the word, conventional jargon has given the name of "vocabulary control." Vocabulary control means nothing more than that the indexer identifies synonyms, or phrases of equivalent meaning, among the index words that he has collected from the text, and having identified synonyms, either lists under each all the references given under the others, or assembles all the references at one term only and makes cross references from the others.

Of the various features that contribute to the practical utility of a book index, none is more important than synonym control. Two questions arise in this connection to which no easy answers can be given. The first is: How does one spot synonyms, or what can be done to ensure that some synonyms are not missed but entered as if they stood for different concepts? The rule-of-thumb method is to notice or remember that there was another word which meant the same thing, but the larger the index the greater the load placed on memory and the more synonyms will slip through the net. The only device for really checking synonymy of terms is classification. Classification is simply the ordering of terms into a systematic pattern of likeness of meaning, so that terms that mean nearly the same are close together. Each term in the index is assigned to its proper place in the classification, and when one finds himself wanting to put one term into a position already occupied by another term there is the evidence of synonymy. It is a formidable task to have to make a classification and then try to fit every index term into it. There is however no other way of systematic checking for synonymy. The making of classifications is a matter about which librarians have been greatly exercised for a long time, but no existing ready-made classification seems ideal as it stands, for the purpose of synonym control. The basic technique for constructing classifications is not difficult to acquire, and becomes easier with practice.[3]

The second question that arises in synonym control is this: If I decide to prefer one term and make cross references from the others, which do I prefer? If one is indexing the work of a single author, that author's preference will surely prevail, but if one is indexing a composite work of multiple authorship or is doing bibliographical indexing, the problem is not always so simply resolved. Attempts have been made in some scientific fields to standardize terminology, but these standards often go against strong conventional preferences. This is particularly the case in chemistry where considerable steps toward systematization of nomenclature have been taken, but where also the briefer so-called trivial names strongly persist in the literature. The names of technical processes often take a long time to settle, and the indexer is frequently called on to make a decision long in advance of a conventional preference. An example that comes to mind is the bulking process applied to yarns to give them softness to the touch, apparent elasticity, and varied thermal insulation properties. The process is variously called bulking, crimping, false twisting, texturing. It recently appeared that texturing was winning the day, but there is now a new variant, "texturizing."

The logical names do not always prevail over the more superficial ones. "Hovercraft" is firmly ascendant in Britain for a certain novel type of vehicle, despite the existence of two other names which refer to more fundamental properties. "Air cushion vehicle" is logically prefer-

[3]Vickery, B. C. *Faceted Classification*. London, Aslib, 1960.

able, because it refers to a more concrete attribute of the vehicle, and there are other vehicles which are not hover-craft that nevertheless hover. Perhaps even more to be pre-ferred is "ground effect machine," which had a good start in the literature but which is rapidly falling out of favor. The direction in which technical advances are made sometimes helps to establish a conventionally preferred name: Hovercraft may eventually give way to Air Cushion Vehicle. The same air cushion principle is now finding applications elsewhere, for instance in the handling of delicate strip material at the strip mills, but it is not possible to bring the word Hover-craft into a name for these air cushion bearings, though they have been called Hover Pulleys. Little more can be said about correct choice of synonym except that, like nearly every other indexing problem, it becomes harder in propor-tion to the width of subject field being covered.

So far this chapter has dealt with two levels of sophistica-tion in indexing. At the first level, the essential operation was one of manipulating given *words*. At the second the concern has moved on to the listing of *concepts*, by means of words it is true, but by means of words to which synonym control has been applied, so that the index user no longer needs to depend upon the particular term under which he first thinks of looking. At both of these levels there is also the underlying question of what is a significant term and what is not.

Both of these levels in various admixtures are characteris-tic of indexes to books by individual authors, but as a rule the better sort of book index is the one operating on level two. The third level is normally appropriate to indexes to compilative or collective works with contributions from various authors, and to bibliographical subject indexes. It is distinguished from level two in that it includes connective references between related terms in the index.

It is easy to see why this is generally appropriate only to the indexing of material of heterogeneous origin. In the text by an individual author, the arrangement of the material itself is determined by the relationships between the various parts of the subject that the author thinks important. The writer doubts if it is part of the indexer's job to indicate other relationships, or even to reproduce those implicit in the arrangement of the text. But different considerations apply in the case of indexes to heterogeneous material or to the contents of large numbers of individual items such as scientific papers.

Now anyone who sets about constructing a network of relational cross references quickly realizes that there is no end to this process, and the network very quickly becomes a maze. The problem is how to put a limit on the process, and the general answer is to confine the work to showing one type of relationship only. For most purposes the most useful relationship is that of inclusion. Make connective references from one term to others included within its meaning, as from INTERNAL COMBUSTION ENGINE to DIESEL ENGINE and GAS TURBINE or from FISHING VESSEL to TRAWLER, from POLYAMIDE FIBER to NYLON. But here again we do not go very far before being beset by difficulties. For a given term, there are usually several possible, wider including terms. For instance, one might legitimately insist that GAS TURBINE should have a cross reference from the inclusive term TURBINE, and NYLON might equally well be regarded as coming under THERMOPLASTICS, as under POLY-AMIDE FIBERS. So the indexer needs not only to limit himself to inclusion relationships but also a device to help him sort out the inclusion relationships themselves. Such a device is found in classification schemes, for these are essentially attempts to lay out multidimensional relationships in linear form.

Thus classification is relevant to indexing in two ways. First of all on what was called level two, as a helpful means of detecting synonyms, and now as providing a basis for a network of relational references. Once again it must be repeated that this particular aspect of the indexing task, like most others, is easier when the subject field being covered is narrow. The wider the field, the harder the task.

Now let us turn to another aspect of indexing work which in some degree applies to all fields but is especially prominent in scientific and technical material. Most of the concepts that one wishes to index are composite in character, that is to say they cannot be expressed in a single word, but require a phrase, sometimes something almost approaching a sentence. For example, DROP FORGING. DROP FORGING HAMMERS. VIBRATIONS OF DROP FORGING HAMMERS. DAMPING THE VIBRATIONS OF DROP FORGING HAMMERS. Let us concentrate on the most complex example:

DAMPING VIBRATIONS OF HAMMERS FOR DROP FORGING

Why can't one index the subject in just that form? The answer is not that the subject is too long to express: subjects of that degree of complexity are sought by people who consult indexes, though they may not start with exactly those words or that order of words in mind. The phrase as it stands is unacceptable for indexing purposes because it contains prepositions which are always nonsignificant words. So let us then take out the prepositions: We are left with

DAMPING, VIBRATIONS, HAMMERS, DROP FORGING

This composite term entry remains intelligible even when the prepositions are dropped because the order in which the five significant terms appeared in the natural language phrase is still retained. If the indexer starts shifting the five terms round very much, he soon begins to lose the sense, for very good reasons. The damping is directly related to the vibrations and only related to the hammer through vibrations, so that there is a linear chain of relationships. If one starts to tangle up the straight chain, then intelligibility suffers. But you will insist quite rightly that the index should provide a lead-in to this composite concept from each of the significant terms, VIBRATIONS, HAMMERS, DROP, and FORGING. How does one manage this and yet avoid the chain tangling mentioned? There are two (and perhaps more than two) fairly simple ways of doing this. Let us recall the technique of the KWIC index, and rotate the terms as follows:

Entry 1
 DAMPING, VIBRATIONS, HAMMERS, DROP FORGING
Entry 2
 VIBRATIONS, HAMMERS, DROP FORGING/ DAMPING
Entry 3
 HAMMERS, DROP FORGING/DAMPING, VI- BRATIONS
Entry 4
 DROP FORGING/DAMPING, VIBRATIONS, HAMMERS
Entry 5
 FORGING/DAMPING, VIBRATIONS, HAM- MERS, DROP

The sense in these cases remains reasonably clear because the linear chain has been broken once only, though entry 5 suggests that making a break between a term and a qualifying epithet may never be justified. A variant of this method that is sometimes used is the following:

| | |
|---|---|
| DAMPING | Damping, Vibrations, Hammers, Drop forging |
| VIBRATIONS | Damping, Vibrations, Hammers, Drop forging |
| HAMMERS | Damping, Vibrations, Hammers, Drop forging |
| DROP | Damping, Vibrations, Hammers, Drop forging |
| FORGING | Damping, Vibrations, Hammers, Drop forging |

One point to be noticed is that the linear chain may be used equally well in either direction:

FORGING, Drop, Hammers, Vibrations, Damping

In this case to translate the index entry into natural language, one reads the elements backwards, Damping *of* Vibrations *of* Hammers *for* Drop forging. The backwards form is used in the *British Technology Index*. Where it is an economy to use references in the index instead of direct entries, the problem can be approached in another way. In the following illustration the reversed form just mentioned will be used though the forward form will do equally well. The full entry is:

FORGING, Drop, Hammers, Vibrations, Damping

Next references are made as follows from each of the other four significant terms:

DAMPING, Vibrations, Hammers, Drop forging. *See* FORGING, Drop, Hammers, Vibrations, Damping
VIBRATIONS, Hammers, Drop forging. *See* FORGING, Drop, Hammers, Vibrations
HAMMERS, Drop forging. *See* FORGING, Drop, Hammers
DROP FORGING. *See* FORGING, Drop

The point to notice here is that only the first of the above references details the complete concept. The others are generic references, the import of which is that *something* on DROP FORGING, not necessarily a comprehensive account, is recorded in the index.

This is a very sketchy glance at the problem of ordering the elements of composite concepts which should be cited in indexes. The practical solution is not always as simple and straightforward as in the illustration given, but on the other hand it is not impossibly complex once its measure has been taken. The indexing in the *British Technology Index* is fairly sophisticated as indexing goes, yet here we have been able to reduce most of our problems to a dozen basic situations. The residual issues, however, are often of very considerable difficulty.

Perhaps this chapter could end with a mention of three persistent danger points that call for the utmost watchfulness.

The first of these relates to homonyms, which abound in technical literature, because of the ingrained habit of electrical, electronic, nuclear, and even chemical engineers, of borrowing words from the field of mechanical engineering and assigning them by analogy to new objects and processes. Thus the electrical engineer has taken over FILTER and BRIDGE to mean a particular circuit, and the electronic engineer has, of course, TUBES or VALVES only very tenuously related to the tubes and valves met in mechanical engineering. The chemical engineer "cracks" hydrocarbons, and the nuclear engineer contemplates the "burn up" of uranium, though the process is fundamentally different from what is meant by burning in other contexts. The practical answer is to avoid alphabetical interspersion of homonyms of this kind:

BRIDGES, A. C.
BRIDGES, arch
BRIDGES, bascule
BRIDGES, decks
BRIDGES, electrical
BRIDGES, girders

This can be improved by inserting a qualifier:

BRIDGES, arch
BRIDGES, bascule
BRIDGES, decks
BRIDGES, electrical
BRIDGES, electrical, A. C.
BRIDGES, girders

However, there are still blocks of material on structural bridges sandwiched in the electrical ones. A further improvement can be made by attaching to the introduced qualifier term some punctuation device with an arbitrarily assigned ordinal value greater than Z. But arbitrarily assigned order, even of the simplest kind, leaves wide-open pitfalls to the user who is usually prepared to accept the burden of knowing A to Z order, but not one jot or tittle more. The more difficult homonym problems are met in BTI in this way:

BRIDGES, decks

BRIDGES, electrical. *See* after the last subheading on structural bridges

BRIDGES, girder

BRIDGES, Zurich

BRIDGES, electrical

BRIDGES, structural *See* subheadings preceding BRIDGES, electrical

The second general difficulty which calls for watchfulness is that connected with the subject naming of pieces of equipment so novel in character that at the time of indexing they have no settled name. It may be instructive to consider generally how objects are named. Any object has the basic properties of shape, material, function, and sometimes method of working. Established names of man-made articles usually refer to function. As an example, a familiar object comprising a thread of mercury in a graduated capillary tube is called a thermometer in reference to its function. It is not called a mercury capillary, or a mercury expansion column, or anything of that sort. The moral for indexers is fairly clear. A new, as yet unnamed object is to be described primarily by its function, or by its shape if its function is multifarious. Thus a new textile fabric would be designated in BTI as

CLOTHING (Function) Fabrics (Form) Polyester fiber (Material)

If it is used for a variety of purposes beside clothing it will be entered as

FABRICS (Form) Polyester fiber (Material)

If it is a question of a new material only, which might be made in the form of either yarns, cords, or fabrics, then we enter simply under the chemical name of the material:

POLYESTER FIBER

The third problem is the most intractable of all. Many technical objects and processes possess properties that are nearly always applicable, taken for granted, and therefore not mentioned, until a new development arises in which the object or process turns up with this normally-taken-for-granted-property absent. For example, nearly all the literature on welding is actually on fusion welding, that is to say on welding in which solid metal is converted to the liquid state by heating. This fusion property is taken for granted until a new technique is devised which does not involve actual melting of metal. At some stage then one has to go back and change the entry WELDING to WELDING, fusion. The difficulty is to know how soon, after what delay, to do this. Another concept in technical literature which often illustrates the same difficulty is that of METAL. Many names of processes imply metal nearly but not quite all the time. MACHINING as used in the technical literature nearly always means the machine forming of metal, but it can be extended to wood, glass, and plastics. WELDING and CASTING usually, but again not quite always, imply metal. The printing trade journals often talk of PRINTING when they actually mean letterpress printing, and if one follows this in indexing he is never sure whether material under PRINTING is about printing generally (letterpress, lithography, gravure, and so on) or about letterpress alone. Perhaps as a general rule it is preferable in the long run to err on the side of pedantry.

The stratum of snags and difficulties that the writer has attempted very sketchily to explore, is that which appears once one has cleared essential questions of definition, of the meaning of words, out of the way. Because science and technology deal proportionately with more concrete and definite topics than do other fields, this layer of difficulty is reached earlier in scientific and technical indexing than in the humanities field. However, it is to be found in indexing of all kinds.

This paper has made little reference to mechanized indexing except marginally. Computers can already produce indexes of a kind, but machines will not realize their full potentialities in this field until indexing technique itself has been systematized and reduced to rule, to a greater extent than is the usual case in today's common practice. Machines behave logically, but cannot exercise discretion. The first step in any useful man-machine partnership in producing indexes is to define precisely the limits of discretion.

## 10

# MEDICAL INDEXING

JOHN L. THORNTON

The indexing of medical books, like that of other works, demands primarily an adequate knowledge of indexing in general. There are many varieties of technique, various materials employed, and numerous ways of setting about the task, but only experience can guide the indexer to the methods that best serve his purpose. Certain rules observed by the beginner will be dispensed with as experience is gained. Always the standard to be aimed at is the best possible index for the work in hand.

## Terminology

The indexing of medical and similar specialist books is complicated by the intricacies of terminology. Indexers unfamiliar with this are liable to serious error, whereas those acquainted with medical literature can save themselves many pitfalls. That one word "medicine" covers so many subdivisions, which in turn impinge on other branches of science, technology, sociology, and all the other branches of knowledge, that it is impossible for any one person to be intimately acquainted with the terminology peculiar to every speciality. The anatomist will employ names of the bones, nerves, arteries, and so on, but even these are not static. They have changed considerably even during the present century, and so the indexer must be on guard.

Other preclinical subjects include physiology, biochemistry, pharmacology, biology, and physics, most of these being encountered again when clinical subjects are considered. Anatomy allied to surgery becomes surgical anatomy; biochemistry comes to the aid of the pathologist, and in diagnosis; while pharmacology forms the basis of medical treatment. The use of isotopes and radiotherapy necessitates the cooperation of the physicist with the physician and surgeon, and there is additional cooperation between the clinical departments. All this tends to make medical books most difficult to index, for the mixture of terminologies can confuse even the specialist. A general textbook on medicine may cover the diagnosis and treatment of all diseases, and will necessitate a very full index. It will obviously be used as a reference book, and should have a comprehensive and precise index. By this is meant that it should direct any inquirer to the exact passage he requires. If he is checking up the effect of penicillin in diphtheria, he should find it under both "Penicillin in diphtheria," and "Diphtheria, penicillin in." He should not discover "Penicillin" followed by three rows of figures, or "Diphtheria, treatment of" followed by the first page number of a lengthy section that includes a paragraph devoted to penicillin. Reference books in particular need detailed indexes; and since it is very difficult to say that a given book cannot possibly be used for reference purposes, every book should be so provided.

As stated earlier, every book to be indexed must receive individual consideration: For whom is it intended? What is its arrangement? Sample its contents. *But*, if it is a medical book, do *not* attempt to read it through. The chances are that the indexer would be even more confused if he did so, besides losing several days of precious time. The publisher will be eagerly awaiting the index, the final step before the book can go to press. If one is limited to a certain number of pages, he must plan accordingly, otherwise the publisher may cut out entries to make the index fit the allotted space. The indexer must submit the size of index the publisher requests—and deserves!

# Types of Medical Literature

Medical literature, as indeed most forms of literature, can be divided into certain types. These will now be considered, and examples given for each type, mostly without comment.

*Encyclopedias.* These are usually in several volumes with the articles in the text arranged alphabetically. In spite of this arrangement an index is essential. If each volume is separately indexed, these can be cumulated to form one index to the entire work, and one that will probably necessitate a separate volume. By the time the work is completed the indexes to the individual volumes will have little value, and unless publication is spread over several years their initial inclusion may have been unnecessary. Each serves as a guide to the contents of one volume only, and is liable to mislead inquirers who may not appreciate this fact.

An example of this type of literature is *British Surgical Practice*, Volume 1, covering "Abdominal emergencies" to "Autonomic nervous system," published in 1947. There is a table of contents, and each section begins with a list of the subjects treated therein. These headings have been carried over in the index, which is set up so as to exasperate any reader. Some of the main headings cover several pages, and the subheadings, sub-subheadings, and so on, meander across the page in a most confusing manner. It is easier to find most things by direct reference to the text. The cumulative index to the eight volumes was published in 1951, and assumed double-column form. This is easier to consult, but is still inadequate and contains some strangely worded entries. For example:

Under "After-care, post-operative," we find entries such as: "flatus, of"; "hiccup, in"; "pain, of"; "restlessness, of"; "vomiting, of"; and finally at the end of the "After-care" entries: "work, return to!" An odd inversion of words throughout the index results in the following samples:

Anaesthesia, Rammstedt operation, for
Aneurysm, scalp of
Arthritis, treatment, arthrodesis, objects of

> Artificial limbs, training in use of, walking sticks with
> Bed-clothes, tight, protracted illness, in
> Beer, gout, in
> Carcinoma, orbit, of
> Diet, anus, artificial, patients with, for

Some of these appear facetious, but they are no joke to the one searching for specific entries; and they are but a few examples from a thoroughly inadequate index.

The companion *British Encyclopaedia of Medical Practice*, 2d ed., began publication in 1950, and is equally lavish. The index to each volume meanders across the complete page, and the cumulative index is introduced by an announcement that "the index has undergone the same thorough process of editorial revision as has been the case with the volumes of text." Unfortunately, it is little better than that to the surgery volumes. The following random examples are typical:

> Child, New Zealand, welfare measures in
>     rights of, declaration of
> Cramp, pregnancy in
> Cyst, distension, breast, of
> Diet, children, for
>     cirrhosis of liver, in

A medical encyclopedia needs an index; but if the entries are arranged by standard headings, e.g., diagnosis, etiology, pathology, treatment, and so on, there is no need to overload the index by including as subheadings every disease excluded in differential diagnosis, every drug tried and found useless, and every bone, muscle, nerve, and blood vessel encountered in an operation. Such inclusion could result in an entire page of index entries referring the inquirer to the same page of text. As stated before, it is easier to consult the main article and either trace the required section by means of the summary at the head of the chapter, or thumb through the article to find the appropriate heading.

*Textbooks.* The general textbooks of medicine are extensive tomes covering a wide field. Price's *Textbook of the*

*Practice of Medicine* (1956) has 1,688 pages of text, a 14-page appendix, and an index of 85 pages in double columns. The last named is well set out, the main entries are printed in bold type, and it can be used for quick-reference purposes. If one looks at the index to a volume devoted to a special branch of medicine, he will notice that some of the sub-headings of the more comprehensive books now become main entries. For example, Davidson's *Practical Manual of Diseases of the Chest* has entries under "Abscess of lung"; "Anatomy"; "Flat chest"; "Palpitation"; "Radiology"; and "Vital capacity." It does *not* have any entries under "Chest," because the rule is to avoid making entries under the subject of the entire book. This rule should be observed in fields other than medicine, and biography suggests itself as an example. In the index, under the name of the bio-graphee there should, theoretically, be no entries, but few indexers can resist subheadings such as: ancestry; birth; baptism; education; marriage; children; and death. These would look strange as main entries in the index, and would usually have to be qualified by the words "of (followed by the name of the biographee)." In some biographies the name of the subject appears in the index followed by an extensive synopsis of the book, possibly in chronological order, and may cover several pages. This latter is not good indexing.

Scientific literature tends to include numerous references to the work of predecessors in the field, either in the form of footnotes, lists at the end of chapters, or bibliographies at the end of the text. When the latter is included, and is arranged alphabetically by the authors' names, it may not seem necessary to include a separate index of authors or of names. But ideally such indexes should be provided in every serious scientific book intended for the research worker, especially as there may be references in the text to the work of other people not included in the bibliography, and joint authors will be almost untraceable unless they are indexed. Librarians are often requested to search for refer-ences which a reader has seen in a book, but which are not included in an index. And often a reader who has noticed a reference in the bibliography wants to read about it in the text, but is unable to locate it.

A model for indexes both of authors and of subjects is Marshall's *Physiology of Reproduction*, Volume 1, part 2 of which was published in 1960. An extensive bibliography covers several pages at the end of each chapter. Following the final bibliography of 31 pages, we have an "Index of Authors" in three columns covering 20 pages, which includes references to authors mentioned in the text as well as in the bibliography. Unfortunately, under some names appear as many as eighty page numbers, but to differentiate further between these entries would swell the author index beyond reason. The "Index of Authors" is followed by a "Subject Index" in double columns covering 24 pages, the subheadings being run-on to save space. This volume is adequately indexed, and could serve as a model to scientists, authors, and indexers.

Monographs on special subjects are most difficult to index, for, as the terminology becomes more complex, the more specialized the work becomes. Terminological inconsistencies and the continual additions to medical terminology cause confusion. In bacteriology and virology, for example, there is disagreement regarding classification, which means that more than one term may represent the same organism. Indexers should always employ the terminology used by the author, with cross references from alternatives given and from terms obviously requiring mention. But they should neither look up in the dictionary every term in the text nor attempt to provide entries for every synonym, pseudonym, trade name, and derivative.

*Pharmacopoeias.* Names of drugs present their problems and are mainly encountered in books on therapeutics, pharmacology, and the sections of more general works devoted to these topics. Most pharmaceutical preparations have synonyms, and proprietary preparations in particular have various names for (practically) the same thing. For example, in Martindale's *Extra Pharmacopoeia*, Volume 1

(1958), the following alternatives appear under Hexamine: Hexamin; Methenamine; Hexamethylenamine; Aminoform; Formin; Formamine; Urisol; Uritone; and Urotropine. Proprietary preparations containing hexamine are given as Cystopurin; Metramine; Mictasol; Saltetramine; Uralysol; Uraseptine; Urogenenine. These trade names are often followed by the names of their respective manufacturers in parentheses. Indexers do not need to look up *all* the synonyms and trade names for drugs mentioned in books being indexed, but they should make entries for those mentioned by the author, and should recognize the connection between them.

*Journals.* Medical periodicals are vitally important to the research worker. They provide up-to-date information that might take years to appear in books, and their contents should be made readily available to readers by means of adequate indexes. Minimum requirements for such indexes have been laid down by the Society of Indexers in "Standards for Indexes to Learned and Scientific Periodicals," *The Indexer*, Vol. 2, 1960–1961, pp. 63–64. Some medical journals have separate author and subject indexes, and periodicals carrying abstracts may have separate author and subject indexes to these as well, making four indexes in all. Where this appears desirable, the indexes should be clearly signposted to avoid confusion. Many medical journals are inadequately indexed. They rely upon lists of contents, or have indexes compiled merely from words used in the titles of articles. Furthermore, whereas in books separate bibliographical entries for authors quoted in the text and in lists of references are considered useful, medical journals generally do not include this feature. What is useful in monographs surely should be equally important in periodicals.

Cumulative indexes to runs of periodicals are valuable to librarians and research workers, and five-, ten-, or twenty-year cumulations to certain journals are published. These are sometimes issued at extra cost to subscribers, and since libraries must be the chief purchasers, only journals having wide circulations can afford to issue these costly items. Indexers who regularly compile indexes to journals from year to year can save their entries to each volume and use them for cumulations, although careful editing is always required. Terminology changes rapidly, and an index covering a period of fifty years or more would call for a thorough knowledge of those changes.

Indexes are intended as guides to the material contained in a book, journal, or similar item, and are included to assist the reader to find material as quickly as possible. Time saving is particularly important in medicine and science, and only good indexes really save time. A publisher should ensure that the index is as good as the text of the book he is issuing. If the author is unable to provide this essential part of the book, the publisher should arrange for its compilation by a competent indexer and make suitable financial arrangements for this, either by charging the cost to the author or by including this expense in his own costing. This latter is probably the best solution, particularly in the case of multiple author books. The entire onus of providing an adequate index to every book would appear to rest with the publisher. Purchasers who find books without indexes should return them to the publishers, just as they would take kettles lacking lids back to the shop. The article is incomplete, and for many purposes useless.

One most important aspect of indexing any subject is the choice of the correct word as the key word. This also depends to a certain extent upon the knowledge of the nomenclature of the subject being indexed. The arrangement of the other words in the entry is important, too. These two features can best be illustrated in the following examples; it is easy to spot the mistakes of others, and not difficult to make the same errors unwittingly!

The following entries appear in the index to R. Prosser White's *Occupational Affections of the Skin*, 2d ed. (1920). The indexes were compiled by the author's secretary, who is mentioned for her "excellent work." There are 289 pages of text, an index of subjects covering 63 pages, and a further

"Index of authorities" to which 6 pages are devoted. Sixty-nine pages suggest a very adequate index for a book of this size, but no index should be judged by the number of pages it fills. In fact, this one includes entries for all journals mentioned by title in the text as sources of references, and many authors' names are included in the index of subjects, even though there is a separate index of authorities. Furthermore, the indexer had the knack of picking the wrong word for her entries, and the results are sometimes ludicrous:

> Anatomical tubercle from animals or human cadaver in physicians, veterinary surgery, bacteriologists, dissecting-room and post-mortem attendants, nurses, undertakers, butchering, and smoke-drying trades
> Appearance of occupational dermatosis
> Author's alcoholic paint. [This and several other entries refer to items appertaining to the author of the book!]
> Bursa, tale of a
> Changes of acid around hair follicles
> Confusion in nomenclature
> Dangers, heavy oil
> Difference between acid and caustic alkali burns
> Dryness as obstacle to work
> Earliest symptoms
> French laundry-women, callosities of
> Harm of alternating heat and cold
> Heels from walking or standing, callosities on
> Hot offending substances
> Surgeons, agents which irritate
> Sweet orange worker's irritation
> To render colours fast
> Writer's case of photographer's dermatitis
> ———— cramp and pressure
> ———— observations of mechanics and female employees incapacitated by cutting compounds
> ———— use of alcohol

When faced with indexing a book on an unfamiliar subject, one should glean information from the book itself, use a book on the same subject with an adequate index as his guide, and consult a dictionary for definitions. He should use a standard British or American dictionary for the spelling, according to the market served, but if the book is to be marketed in both countries suitable cross references are needed. Better still, since cross references sometimes take up more space than would the page numbers, duplicate the entries.

Preliminary notes at the head of an index can assist readers to appreciate the method of arrangement, and explain any unusual features introduced. Symbols for abbreviations will also be looked for here. Where more than one index is included, the nature of each is printed at the top of every page, not only to avoid confusion, but to show that more than one type of index is included.

Medical indexing cannot be taught in one chapter, but some of the pitfalls can be pointed out, the intricacies involved indicated, and certain solutions and examples suggested. Basic indexing technique is essential; a knowledge of the terminology is most helpful; shortcomings can be overcome by experience.

# 11

## LEGAL INDEXING

A. R. HEWITT

The basic principles of indexing apply to any subject, and a chapter devoted to a specialist field must of necessity be confined to peculiarities associated therewith. In the space available here, it will not be possible to discuss all the problems that may arise in the task of indexing in the field of law, which is a vast one with an extensive literature. It is proposed, therefore, to confine this chapter to a survey, in general terms, of the types of literature to be indexed, to examples in the choice of headings and subheadings, and to mentioning some of the problems to be met.

## Categories of Legal Indexing

The indexing of law books may usefully be divided into three categories as follows:

1. Indexing for the lawyer—that is to say, the indexing of practitioners' text-books and works of reference, including the vast legal encyclopedias, collections of statutes, digests, etc., works which would not normally be used outside the profession (although there is a tendency to include such works in public reference libraries)
2. Indexing for a particular class of "informed" reader
3. Indexing for the layman

Works for students may be included in categories 1 or 2 as appropriate.

The expression "indexing for the lawyer" does not call for any elaboration, except, perhaps, to point out that the practicing lawyer is a critical user of indexes; generally he knows what he is looking for and the appropriate headings under which to look. He is often very familiar with a particular book because of constant use or by its reputation, and he knows pretty well that it does contain what he needs. If the index does not lead him to his point quickly and concisely, it is a disappointing and inadequate piece of work. By "indexing for a particular class of informed reader" is meant the indexing of law books written specially for members of particular callings, persons without legal qualifications or training, e.g., the law relating to accountancy, companies, contracts, commercial practices, insurance, and so on, intended for company secretaries and business men; banking law for bank managers and clerks; law relating to architecture, building, surveying, etc., intended for architects and surveyors; ecclesiastical or church law for the cleric, and so on. The third category, "indexing for the layman," is self-explanatory; here may be placed the "popular" books written in an easily understandable style on some particular aspect of the law for the man in the street, law for the householder, the motorist, the shopkeeper, and so on.

There is still another class of reader to be mentioned, namely, university undergraduates or postgraduates. Their reading ranges over categories 1 and 2, but a number of books are published especially for their use, books written with an academic bias. The indexing of such works presents no particular problem, and the indexer competent to index works in category 1 could quite easily undertake the indexing of "academic" works.

The indexing of practitioners' law books is a very highly specialized task, and the field is a limited one. It is restricted to certain classes of indexers who must either have legal qualifications (that is to say, they must be lawyers or graduates in law) *plus* indexing ability, or possess a sound knowledge of the law and legal terms obtained after long association with the legal profession. Here are included law librarians and persons holding senior editorial positions in the great legal publishing houses; such persons must also, obviously, be able to index. Generally speaking, the indexer without these qualifications or experience would not be called upon to undertake indexing of books in the first category. Any indexer, however, might well be called upon to index material in the second and third categories.

A few words, by way of further introduction, about the terms "common law," "statute law," and "case law," may assist the would-be legal indexer. The common law of England is the unwritten law, that is to say, a body of law which has grown out of custom and usage over the centuries; the written law is the statute law, that is to say, laws enacted by the legislature and embodied in statutes. Case law, or, as it is sometimes called, "judge-made law," is the judicial interpretation in the courts of both common and statute law, interpretation made necessary because of uncertainty or ambiguity. Many cases become known as "leading cases"; they are precedents made in the higher courts and must generally be followed in lower courts.

A legal work on a specific subject usually deals with every aspect of that subject and will embrace common law, statute law, and case law. Two good examples of subjects which contain much common law are the law of highways and the law of nuisance. There are many others, of course. Some branches of law (which might be designated "modern" law) have no common-law origin and consist only of statute law and case law, for example the law relating to town and country planning, or to income tax.

Another type of law book is that devoted to a single statute. Legislative output in recent years has reached prodigious proportions, and some statutes are of such complexity and of such far-reaching effect that there is need for a work thereon to be published as soon after their passing as possible. Such a book consists of the statute itself with annotations, commentary, and index. It usually has to be rushed out in the shortest possible time and, once again, the indexer is expected to prepare the index in less than the shortest time. But here a lot of preliminary work can be done by using the final draft of the Bill.

Some works are devoted to commentaries on collections of leading cases in specific fields, but they do not present indexing problems different from other law books.

To conclude these introductory remarks, mention must be made of the encyclopedic work, namely, the comprehensive legal encyclopedia covering the whole body of the law, the collection of Statutes of the Realm, State Codes, the mammoth Digest of Cases, or the collection of Forms and Precedents, each running perhaps to 20, 30, 40, or more volumes, each volume needing an individual index, to be followed by a comprehensive index of the whole work.

As stated in the opening chapter, a counsel of perfection for learner indexers is that the work to be indexed should first be read through before putting pen to slip (or card). This might be possible in the case of a small popular work for the layman or student, but not when one has in front of him a standard practitioners' book running to upwards of 1,000 pages. The indexer should, of course, thumb through the work so as to familiarize himself with the subject and its peculiarities as well as with the arrangement or sequence adopted by the author or editor in its compilation. Having done this and placed at his elbow a good law dictionary the indexer is ready to commence work.

## Reference to Cases and Statutes by Name

Law books for the practitioner and the "informed" non-lawyer will contain many references to statutes by title and to reported cases by name. Such references are the authorities cited by authors and editors, and normally appear in footnotes. These latter are to be fully indexed, but the short titles of statutes or the names of cases are not included in the index (except in unusual circumstances not considered here). These citations are listed in separate tables, known as the "table of cases" and the "table of statutes." They normally appear at the beginning of the book in the following forms:

| *Table of Cases* | Page |
|---|---|
| Abbott v. Stratton (1846) 9 I.Eq.R. 233; 3 Jo. & Lat. 603; 39 Digest 57, 685 | 238(e) |
| Abbott v. Sullivan [1953] 1 K.B. 189; [1952] 1 All E.R. 226; [1952] 1 T.L.R. 133 | 8(e) |
| Aberdeen Rail. Co. v. Blaikie Bros. (1854) 2 Eq.Rep. H.L.; 23 L.T.o.s. 315; 1 Macq. 461 | 191 |
| Bailey v. Macauley (1849) 13 Q.B. 815; 14 Jur. 80 | 230 |
| Baines v. Ewing (1866) L.R. 1 Exch. 320; 4 H. & C. 511; 35 L.J. Ex. 194 | 209(m) |
| Chapman v. Smith [1907] 2 Ch. 97; 76 L.J.Ch. 394; 96 L.T. 662 | 236 |

The abbreviation figures refer to the volume of reports in which the case is reported. In America, references would be given to the National Reporter System or to the State Reports or to both.

| *Table of Statutes* | |
|---|---|
| 15 & 16 Vict. | |
| c. 76 Common Law Procedure Act, 1852 | 2, 33 |
| s. 13 | 33 |
| s. 18 | 7 |
| c. 79 Inclosure Act, 1852 | 301 |
| s. 17 | 18 |
| 16 & 17 Geo. 5 | |
| c. 7 Bankruptcy (Amend.) Act, 1926 | 245 |
| c. 11 Law of Property (Amend.) Act, 1926 | |
| s. 7 | 376 |
| Sch. | 376 |
| 25 & 26 Geo. 5 | |
| c. 24 Finance Act, 1935 | |
| s. 15 | 463 |

Since 1962 the regal years, that is to say, references to 15 & 16 Vict., 16 & 17 Geo. 5, etc., are not used, the statutes being listed by year and chapter number only.

It is not so common a practice in America as in England to provide tables of statutes, but where such a table is given then it usually lists the Federal Statutes and the U.S. Constitution followed by the Statutes of individual states showing the appropriate section references to the current Consolidation or Code of Statutes in force; statutes passed since the latest Code are given in date order. The indexer is sometimes asked to compile such tables, but more often than not this work is undertaken in the publisher's office, or the author's or editor's professional chambers.

## Choice of Headings and Subheadings

In indexing a work devoted to a single subject, e.g., contracts, copyright, executors, mortgages, and many other obvious titles, the use of the actual subject word as a main heading must be avoided, except in a most general way. This advice may appear trite, but one does meet a number of indexes containing dozens of entries under the subject word of the title of the book, whereas the subheadings thereunder should have been used as main headings. One of the best illustrations of what might appear appropriate subheadings but which should be used as *main* entries is the law of Contract. The indexer must pick out and use as main headings such words as:

    assignment
    breach
    consideration
    discharge
    frustration
    illegality
    performance
    rescission

and not use them as subheadings under the main entry of "Contract." However, there must be *some* entries under the word "Contract," e.g., historical development or origin and other general entries.

One may have, on the other hand, a work dealing with a specific *branch* or *field* of law containing a number of subjects, e.g., commercial law, in which case the indexer would then need to use such words as subheadings under "Contract." Some headings, however, would quite properly be used as subheadings *as well*: for example, "breach," which could be used as a subheading under "Contract" and as a main heading in its own right because, in such a general work as the one mentioned, the word "breach" could apply not only to breach of contract but to breach of covenant, of duty, of trust, of warranty, and so on.

## Singular and Plural of Words

Normally one would not use as index headings *both* the singular and plural forms of a word—either but not both. This is an excellent rule, but one which does not apply in legal indexing. In law the singular word often has a meaning quite different from the plural, and care must be exercised to avoid their combination into what could result in a misleading and ridiculous group of entries. The point will be readily appreciated if one considers the words "damage" and "damages"—words each with a different meaning. Other examples (and there are many) are:

| | |
|---|---|
| Equity | Equities |
| Security | Securities |
| Custom | Customs |
| Pleading | Pleadings |

If both singular and plural forms are used in their different meaning, then *both* must go in the index.

## Double Meanings

Unless the indexer is familiar with the subject or has some knowledge of the law or is able to recognize legal terms, then a trap exists in the use of words with two or more meanings; and here one may take as an example the word "attachment." Apart from its general meanings it possesses two quite different legal interpretations. The first, "attachment of debts," is a process which enables a creditor to obtain satisfaction of his debt from money belonging to his debtor which is in the hands of a third party. Next, "attachment of persons," is a process whereby a person is brought before court for contempt and for ultimate committal to prison. So as to insure no confusion in the index the safest entries are "attachment of debt" and "attachment of persons," each in full, and not

```
attachment
    debt, of
    persons, of
```

Other examples which come to mind are election, fine, franchise, information, issue, ward.

The word *election* means choice—the election of a person to office, particularly to Parliament (or Congress) or to local authorities. The use of the word in equity, although it means choice, has a different implication and is found mostly in the interpretation of wills. Defining it briefly one might say that a beneficiary sometimes has to decide between two devises; he is not permitted to take both, so he must "elect" which of the benefits he will accept.

*Fine* is a word with a number of meanings. Generally it refers to a penalty or punishment, but it also means a penalty not in the criminal sense as well as the discharge of an obligation by means of payment.

*Franchise* has the obvious meaning—the right to vote, but it also means "liberty" or the enjoyment of rights other than to vote.

*Information* in one sense means "knowledge" and in another it is a certain legal process.

*Issue* means child or a legal proceeding.

*Ward* could mean part of a local government area or an infant under guardianship.

These few examples demonstrate how important it is to understand the words used in index headings.

## Phrases as Headings

Phrases are frequently used at length in legal indexing; they are recognized legal expressions and would appear to the lawyer somewhat absurd if broken down in the index.

One must have constantly in mind the needs of the user of the book. As examples there are such terms as "Tenant for life," not "Tenant, life, for"; "Notice of motion," not "Motion, notice of"; "Notice to quit," not "Quit, notice to"; "Execution of judgment," not "Judgment, execution of."

## Maxims and Latin and French Phrases

The law of England (and consequently of the United States) contains much inherited from Roman law, so that Latin maxims frequently occur in legal textbooks. Again, until the seventeenth century the language of the courts was French, and expressions and terms in that tongue are still used. Following are some examples: *caveat emptor*; *estate pur autre vie*; *profit à prendre*; *quantum meruit*; *ratio decidendi*; *rex nunquam moritur*. No attempt should be made to translate them; each must appear in the index as it stands.

## Prepositions

It may sound superfluous to stress the point that the use of prepositions at the beginning of subheadings should be avoided; but clumsy entries of this nature are frequently met. The following is an extract from the index of a published work:

```
Costs
    assisted cases, in
    bill of
        costs of preparation, disallowance
        lodging
    deposit in court pending appeal
    fixed
    High Court scale
    in administrative actions
        garnishee proceedings
    liability of guardian ad litem
    next friend, undertaking by
    of appeals to Court of Appeal
        application for private sale
        discovery
        interrogatories
```

> recovery
> sale of goods seized to pay
> sales of
>> certificate for award on different
>> counsel's fees
>> discretion where none prescribed
>> garnishee proceedings
>> in remitted proceedings
> security for
>> appeals to Court of Appeal
>> by trustee in bankruptcy
>> discovery, of
>> new trial

One notices the use of the words "in" and "of" at the beginning of some of the subheadings. In each case the entries should appear not under "i" or "o" but under the main word, for instance,

> administrative actions, in
> discovery, of
> interrogatories, of
> trustee in bankruptcy, by

Again, the use of prepositions in the body of the entry where it is not strictly necessary should be avoided—"total income, husband and wife, of." Here the word "of" is not essential. On the other hand, proper use must be made of prepositions, and in the correct places, if, without them, ambiguity would result. As an example: the text might refer to the grant of a license by an author to an editor or publisher to use his work, in which case the index entry should read

> author
>> license by, to publish

and not

> author
>> license to publish by

The different interpretations attaching to these examples can be readily appreciated.

## Definition or Meanings

Statutes contain, usually in one of the last sections, interpretations of words and terms used therein. Again, the result of many an action in the courts depends on the judicial interpretation of a word. For these reasons one finds law books full of definitions and these must be included in the index. The appropriate entry usually reads

> embezzlement
> meaning (or meaning of)

In some very large practitioners' works these interpretations *also* appeared grouped together alphabetically under some such heading as "definitions" or "words and phrases." A point to be stressed here is that, in the case of a definition of a *phrase* or *clause* the entry should appear under the first word thereof, and it should *not* be inverted, e.g., "earned income" under "earned"; "lien on share in company" under "lien" and not "share" or "company." The definition is of the whole phrase as used or written and a word out of context has, frequently, quite a different meaning.

## Repetition in the Index of Law in the Text

Index entries are frequently encountered that in themselves provide the answer to the point being searched for by the user, but an index is not a digest and this practice should be avoided. The reader should be directed to the relevant page on which he will find his answer. He does not expect the answer to be actually in the index. (In any case the indexer may have misread the paragraph and thereby made an incorrect statement.) The following is an actual entry in a published index and is a good example of what *not* to include in a legal index:

> husband, presumption that wife entitled to pledge credit for household necessaries

Apart from any other consideration it is a clumsy entry. It should have read

husband
  wife, pledge of credit for necessaries by.

There are always exceptions to rules and occasionally it is difficult to avoid making a statement of law or fact if the law or fact is negative, for example: "There is no common law right on the part of a member of a corporation to vote by proxy." Here the entry should read

proxy, vote by, absence of common law right to

Note the use of the word "absence," rather than "there is no." One should avoid, if possible, the use of "no," "none," and "not."

## Brevity

Brevity in a law index is just as desirable as in any other type of index. Rambling entries not only look ragged and untidy but are irritating to the reader. In a work on election law this entry appears:

service, right to apply to be treated as absent voter by reason of

On turning to the page referred to, at the relevant sentence (under a general heading of "Absent voters") one reads, "A person registered as a service voter may apply." The index entry contains no fewer than thirteen words and refers to a sentence containing only nine words. The entry would better be written as

service voter, absent, application for treatment as

Another example of unnecessary length has already been given above:

pledge of husband's credit.

## Cross References

The adequate use of cross references is essential, and the extent of one's use of them naturally depends on his knowledge of the subject. There is a distinct difference in the use of *See, See also, See under*. Such a reference as "Deed, separation *See* Separation deed" needs no explanation. *See* is a straightforward reference to another heading used by the indexer as better expressing the sense of the entry, e.g., "Testamentary disposition *See* Will," the latter being a heading in more general use. *See also* is used to refer to additional or related headings, e.g., "Negotiable instruments *See also* Bills of exchange; and Check"; "Borough council *See also* Local authority." *See under* is used in a somewhat different sense in that the searcher is told that the subject word for which he is looking is actually used under another heading, e.g., "Taxation of costs *See under* Costs"; that is to say, the word "taxation" is used as a subheading under the heading "Costs," as follows:

Costs
    county court
    high court
    scale of
    taxation of

In most cases a comprehensive law dictionary will help in the selection of allied words or terms even if the book being indexed does not.

## Alphabetization

There are two methods of alphabetization—the word-by-word arrangement and the letter-by-letter arrangement [see pp. 50–53].

New Zealand        Newfoundland

or

Newfoundland       New Zealand

In legal indexing there is no hard-and-fast rule, but in general the word-by-word sequence is preferred.

| | |
|---|---|
| Ex parte | In camera |
| Ex turpi, etc. | In transitu |
| before | before |
| Examination | Incapacity |
| Executor | Inclosure |

In the case of hyphenated words, however, it is usual to follow the letter-by-letter method. [The example given here employs hyphens according to British usage.]

Sub-agent
Submission
Sub-mortgage
Subrogation
Sub-tenant

## Layout of Cards or Slips

Some indexers feel that the layout of an index is not their concern, a point of view not generally shared. The way in which cards or slips are written will materially help the printer, especially in legal indexing where one frequently uses headings that must be subdivided, sub-subdivided, and even sub-sub-subdivided. An example of such entries, taken from a published lawbook index, is given in the appendix to this chapter. Specimen A would necessitate a single column index and the result is most unsatisfactory. Specimen B gives exactly the same set of references but in a manner easy to read and quick to consult.

## Final Comments

The standard of legal indexing varies as in other fields, but perhaps not to quite so great a degree. The foremost law publishers realize that practitioners' books need good and adequate indexes. One house will enjoy a reputation for assuring good indexes to its books and will engage the services of competent legal indexers. Another house will not undertake indexing arrangements, so that authors or editors are obliged to compile the index themselves or employ an indexer. But once a standard work has the reputation of possessing a good index, then succeeding editors of that work usually insure the continuance of that standard by obtaining the services of an experienced indexer. Some publishing houses that only occasionally issue lawbooks do not always appreciate the needs of their readers; then one meets an all too common example of poor and inadequate indexing.

Hopefully, enough has been said here to demonstrate some of the problems met in legal indexing. It is not an easy task, but is one that can, with patience and industry, be learned after careful apprenticeship.

*Appendix: Layout*

### Specimen A

COUNTY COURT, remitted proceedings,
    contract or tort, order as to, appeal against,
                            application for,
                            discretion of court,
                            effect of,
    counterclaim, delivery of statement of,
                further particulars,
    interpleader proceedings,
                under execution order,
    transmission of documents,
    venue,

### Specimen B

County Court
  remitted proceedings
    contract or tort
      order as to
        appeal against
        application for
        discretion of court
        effect of
      counterclaim
        delivery of statement of
        further particulars
      interpleader
        proceedings
        under execution order
      transmission of documents
      venue

# 12

# EDITING OF INDEXES AND THEIR PREPARATION FOR PRESS

G. NORMAN KNIGHT

> When the Indexer comes to the last page of a great book he rejoices to have finished his work; but he will find by experience, when he calculates the arrangement of his materials, that he has scarcely done more than half of what is before him.
>
> Henry B. Wheatley, *How to Make an Index*

Wheatley's warning is necessary for anyone who imagines that once he has made his last index entry all he has to do is sit back, relax, and wait for the check to come along. Two tasks remain to be done, although the writer's experience suggests that usually together they will not consume as much as one half of the time taken so far on the whole job.

First, the index manuscript must be edited and prepared as suitable "copy" for the printer. Then, about a fortnight after one has sent off the fruits of his labors to the publisher he can expect to receive the printed proofs of the index to be read through for any necessary corrections. This matter of proofreading will form the subject of the next chapter, to be followed by a practical exercise.

Before coming to editing proper, perhaps a word or two should be said about the form in which the index manuscript should be sent to the publisher for transmission to the printer. It can either be typewritten on sheets or else sent on the index cards (or slips, including gum slips) on which it was compiled.

If the index is typed—and this will be essential if it has been compiled in an alphabetized notebook—the following rules should be observed:

1. double spacing (except possibly for run-on subheadings) on one side only of the paper
2. ample margins, especially on left of page
3. pages to be numbered consecutively
4. top copy to be sent and carbon copy retained

Printers prefer to work from typed sheets. They often refer to cards (and slips) as "rough copy," for using which they charge extra. The reason is obvious. On the linotype and monotype machines (on which our indexes are typeset) a reading rack is arranged on which the compositor rests his copy. If every time he comes to the end of one card (probably more often than not containing only one or two lines) he has to take it off and replace it with another from the pile on the table, the job is clearly going to take considerably longer.[1]

Instances, however, of a printer's refusing to accept a neat and legible set of index cards are rare. Should this happen, the cards can be pasted onto paper, often as many as ten to the sheet.

Perhaps the writer ought to mention that personally he always uses cards in preference to slips. They are more expensive, but they can often be used three or four times. The writer also likes to have his index always standing in order between alphabetical markers in a special box, so that he can look at once to see whether a subject has occurred before in the book's text and, if necessary, add a subheading or a fresh page reference. He always types the original heading on the card and all subheadings, adding extra page numbers in ink. In this way the index is

[1] But some British printers now use a device which, fitted into the linotype rack, will flick the piled-up cards over as quickly as required.

constantly complete (apart from the final editing) as far as it has gone. And much of the editing is done, so to speak, en route.

In editing an index manuscript one needs chiefly to watch for the following "nine points of editing":

## 1. Alphabetical Arrangement

It is quite a simple matter for a card to have strayed into the wrong order in its own letter of the alphabet or even into a different letter. If it is left there, the compositor will surely print it where it stands and corrections will be necessary in the proofs. Since the cost of such corrections, especially in page proofs, can run into money, the alphabetical arrangement should be carefully checked before being sent on. The next chapter will discuss the cost of such correction.

## 2. Correct Spelling Throughout

This speaks for itself. But perhaps the writer may be allowed a digression which barely concerns editing but does raise a point not much stressed in the foregoing chapters. This is that the indexer is in an ideal position to detect errors and discrepancies in the text of the book he is indexing—discrepancies which may easily have escaped the notice of both author and publisher's reader alike, such as the same name spelled in more than one way.

From his personal experience on various occasions the writer found himself in almost daily telephone communication with the author or publisher regarding queries or suggested corrections—by no means merely of spelling. This is no part of the indexer's job (unless he has been expressly commissioned to correct the proofs). But experience has shown that it is usually welcomed by the publisher's editor, who is not averse to having an additional, unpaid proofreader. Also any indexer who takes pride in his work will wish the text of all books on which he has labored to be as nearly perfect as possible.

## 3. Typography

There is much that wants watching here. All words which are to be in *italics* (e.g., titles of books, periodicals, operas, and long poems; names of ships; foreign words and *See* and *See also*) must be underlined.

See that quotation marks ("quotes") are used when citing titles of: articles in magazines, chapters of books; essays; pictures, sculptures, and songs; shorter poems; and the names of hotels and inns, when these do not form part of a title.

If the main references are to be differentiated by their page numbers' being printed in **boldface,** the latter must be underlined with a wavy line (‿‿‿‿‿‿‿).

Again, if headings must be printed in large and small capitals, then either they must be appropriately marked (as will be explained in the next chapter) or else general instructions can be sent to the printer. These general instructions will be discussed shortly.


## 4. Punctuation

Commas must be correctly and consistently placed. There must be a comma *between* every page reference or group of page references (by "group" is meant for example "138–140"). But, as British Standard 3700:1964 has allowed, the modern tendency is rather to dispense with the use of the comma *before* the first page reference, substituting an appropriate space after the end of the words of headings and subheadings. (But American practice calls for the comma.)

On no account must a comma be used after a main heading which is not followed immediately by page numbers, but only by subheadings. If a run-on system is used, a colon must be placed after the main heading. This very important rule is sometimes ignored, with resulting ambiguity. Thus:

Churches: abbey, 839, 972; basilican, 538; Byzantine, 753; . . .

Now if "Churches" were to be followed by a comma, it might appear that "abbey" was part of the heading and that the first modification was "basilican," so that both the "basilican" and the "Byzantine," and all the other types of church coming after were "abbey churches."

Where the run-on system is adopted for subheadings, as just shown, each subheading must be separated by a semicolon. In the line-by-line system subheadings are taken care of by indentation. For example:

> Churches
> abbey, 839, 972
> basilican, 538
> Byzantine, 753

But the colon should be used instead of a comma when the first subheading is placed on the same line as the heading.

Full stops are not used in an index except (a) to mark an abbreviation, such as "Bro." or "F.R.S."; (b) before *See also*.

## 5. Subheadings

The following rule does not apply to typescript indexes, but only to those submitted on cards or slips, where subheadings may extend to several cards.[2] The main heading will have to be repeated on each of them in order to determine their position in sequence, but should be circled on the second and all subsequent cards. Otherwise it will almost certainly be printed each time, necessitating expensive correction on the proofs.

## 6. Too many page numbers in a row

Sometimes in an index as many as fifty page references can be seen strung in unbroken rows. Such an entry is quite useless for the reader, who might just as well skim through the whole book to find the particular item he is seeking. About seven references should be the absolute limit (except

[2] Observations about cards in this chapter apply equally to slips.

after the subheading "other references"), and fewer are recommended.

Excessive page references can be avoided by the use of subheadings, with a final "other references" for the more trivial items. If a subheading itself has the extra page numbers, then either there can be sub-subheadings or else (and preferably in the case of indexing general literature) just "*See* - - - - -," with the topic itself made into a separate main heading, with its own subheadings.

7.  "See" and "See also"

It is important during editing to make sure that the cross reference does actually appear in the index and has the page numbers following it. Nothing is more infuriating to the index user than either to draw a complete blank or else to find that the cross reference merely refers him back to the original reference.

In his *Making an Index* (Cambridge University Press, 1951), G. V. Carey exemplifies this type of procedure in his own delightful index, written (as he explains) "with his tongue in both cheeks." Thus, we have an entry: "Von Kluck, *see* Kluck, von." But under the latter we merely find: "Kluck, von, *see* Von Kluck." In the text of his pamphlet Carey calls this a "wild goose chase," which he duly indexes under "Wild goose chase" as well as "Goose chase, wild," and "Chase, wild goose." All three are merely followed by "*see* Kluck, von."!

To facilitate ease of research, *See* references should be avoided unless there are more than three page numbers or some subheadings. Thus take the case of a passage on "the electronic indexing of the Dead Sea Scrolls." Here conceivably the following three index entries are indicated, any one of which might equally well be looked up by the researcher:

| | |
|---|---|
| Dead Sea Scrolls, electronic indexing of | 13, 97, 105 |
| Electronic indexing of Dead Sea Scrolls | 13, 97, 105 |
| Indexing of Dead Sea Scrolls, electronic | 13, 97, 105 |

The important thing in editing such entries is to see that all the page numbers are shown in each entry and that they all correspond.

It is also important to insure that there is no conflict between entries and *See also* cross references.

## 8. Scattered Information

Other errors to be looked for while editing the "copy" are instances where information has been split or scattered among synonymous or related headings instead of being grouped under the same heading; or again where similar information has been indexed at different hierarchical levels.

## 9. Preliminary Notes

If special symbols are to be employed, such as certain page numbers being marked to be printed in **bold face type** or *italics* (to denote main references or illustrations, respectively); or the use of *bis* and *ter* after a page number (to denote two or three quite separate mentions of the item on the same page); or the use of (a) or (i) and (b) or (ii) to indicate different columns in the text of the book, then there should be an explanatory note at the beginning of the index giving their meaning. Similarly any other unconventional features should be so explained. This certainly forms part of the editing process.

The following notes which appeared at the top of the index to a recent biography are fairly typical of Preliminary Notes, although perhaps somewhat more extensive than usual:

> The names of Winston Churchill occur on almost every page of the text. To avoid unnecessary overloading, the entry under his name has not been made a table of contents of the entire volume but has been confined to those headings which cannot be readily found under other entries.
>
> Throughout the index his name has been abbreviated to WSC and that of his son, the author, to RSC.

Large and small CAPITALS for a surname denote that it is the subject of a short biography between page xxv and page xxxvi.

Page numbers in **bold type** indicate that more than a few lines are devoted to the subject in the text. Reference numbers in *italics* indicate illustrations or their captions, or maps. *qv* stands for *quod vide* ("which see").

*bis* after a reference number denotes that the item is quite separately mentioned twice on the same page of the text, and *ter* three times. *q.* stands for "quoted"; *passim* denotes that the references are scattered throughout the pages indicated (e.g. 102–7 *passim*).

Sub-headings have been arranged mainly in a chronological order. The method of alphabetical arrangement is word-by-word.

The beginning indexer may ask: Nine points of editing? Surely all this work is not really necessary before the index is submitted? Can it not be sent as it stands and necessary corrections made on the proofs? The answer is: Of course, they could, but the operation might prove enormously expensive and also delay the final production of the book. Some idea of the cost of proof corrections will be given in the next chapter. The whole aim of editing should be to have a manuscript so intelligible and so perfectly prepared that the only mistakes to be corrected in the proofs will be those of the printer.

As with so many other things, speed in editing comes with practice, and the experienced indexer can be found flicking through his cards at a fairly fast rate. Except in the case of the very largest indexes, such as those mentioned in James Thornton's chapter, a single day's work should be ample to carry out the whole process comfortably.

## General Instructions to the Printer

A brief reference to this topic has already been made (page 170). It certainly pays to send with the index manuscript some separate instructions to the printer. If they are put at the top of the typescript (when the index is submitted in this form), they must be circled to show that they are not to be printed. They could include such directions as the following:

1. When paging the proofs, please be sure that, where a subheading extends from one column onto the next, the main heading is repeated at the top of the second column.

[This practice makes all the difference to an index's usefulness and appearance, but is very often omitted unless the printer is reminded.]

2. Print all headings or all main headings in large and small capitals.
3. [For cards and slips only]
   Subheadings are to be run on or, alternatively, printed in line-by-line style.
4. [If subheadings are to be run on]
   Separate subheadings by semicolons.
5. Wherever a main heading is not followed immediately by page numbers but only by subheadings, please see that after the heading a colon is placed.

13

# THE CORRECTION OF INDEX PROOFS

G. NORMAN KNIGHT

If life had a second edition, how would I correct the proofs!

John Clare

Essential though it is, reading the proofs is not the most interesting part of index making. Nevertheless, the writer feels that indexers should always offer to correct the proofs of their indexes and even insist as far as possible upon doing so. And the Society of Indexers does not encourage the making of a separate charge for this service, which is indispensable if the indexer is to have any responsibility for the form in which his index reaches the public. Normally publishers send the proofs without question. Usually two sets are sent, but only one need be returned.

Some time after one has sent off his carefully edited index manuscript (whether in the form of nicely typewritten sheets or of the rubber-banded bundles of index cards or slips on which it was compiled), he may expect to receive the whole thing back together with the printed proofs for his attention. The length of time elapsing before this happens will depend upon the length of the index and how free the printer may be to devote his time to it.

These proofs reach the indexer in one of two forms: they are either long galley sheets, which are not even divided into columns; or else they come in the form of page proofs, which again may be either paged galleys or ordinary pages, but are sometimes bound up elaborately with the text of the book into a rough paperback.

Whole lines can be safely added or deleted on ordinary galleys but this should never be attempted on page proofs without full compensation in the same column. Otherwise every single succeeding page of the index may have to be re-made up, or at the very least until the next letter of the alphabet is reached. In the same way, in the case of a long set of run-on subheadings, the insertion or deletion of a whole word should be avoided except in the last line, since otherwise a resetting of every subsequent line of the entry may be necessary.

Why are such stringent precautions necessary? They are required because of the enormous expense of making corrections on the printed page, regarding which the writer can supply some figures. British printers say that the cost of setting corrections in linotype, including the work of the proofreader, the linotype operator, and the stone hand, comes to as much as three guineas per hour; while the insertion of a single comma, if done as a lone operation, would reasonably take a full half-hour. All this is explained in a useful little sixpenny pamphlet entitled *Author's Corrections Cost Money and Cause Delay*, produced by the British Federation of Master Printers in collaboration with the Publishers' Association. The pamphlet also contains a table of the more commonly used symbols employed in proof correction. Equivalent costs in the United States would be a dollar a line for page proof.

Consequently, at the page-proof stage, trivial verbal amendments are rarely worth while, and when one is tempted he should bear in mind Sir Francis Bacon's dictum: "The most corrected copies are commonly the least correct." The time for making corrections is when editing one's script for the press.

Now for the actual work of proofreading. There are in reality (though not officially) two classes of corrections:

those due to printer's errors and those which are genuine "author's corrections," i.e., due to mistakes in the indexer's original copy—but if he carefully edited and prepared his script for the press, there should be none—or else due to afterthoughts. When correcting the former, the printer's own errors, it is the writer's invariable practice to put a circled note in the margin: "See copy." This is not strictly necessary but it may save unnecessary charges to the publishers.

The proofs will often be found to contain marginal notes from the printer's reader, querying ambiguities, inconsistencies, or possible inaccuracies. If one agrees with the printer's suggestion, he strikes out the question mark. If not, he strikes out the suggested alteration as well.

Sometimes an unfamiliar touch in the proof will turn the indexer to his copy, an examination of which will reveal that the publisher's editor has himself taken a hand by "tampering with" or "improving" (according to the point of view) the script. Such a case calls for the greatest tact, but if the indexer does not consider the amendment to be an improvement, he should at least inquire the reasons for it. He may learn that his own style infringed one of the house rules of the firm concerned.

Proofreading should be carried out by scanning the index, line by line, for possible errors. Each line of the proof should be most carefully checked against the original index "copy" and special care must be taken in checking the page reference numerals since there is a higher rate of typographical errors in numbers than in letters and the mistakes are more damaging. Except in case of doubt, it should rarely be necessary to refer to the text of the book. A commonly adopted method of focusing the attention on one line at a time is to place under it a ruler or sheet of paper, which can be gradually moved downwards.

The question is sometimes asked: Is it necessary to check the accuracy of each page number entry by looking up the appropriate reference in the text? Ideally, of course, that should be done, since the page number references are a vital part of any index. But experience seems to show that very rarely do the page numbers on the proof fail to correspond to those in the copy and that any error (other than the indexer's own) will be due to a new paragraph or two having been inserted in, or an old one deleted from, the book's text at the last moment, without the indexer having been notified. Such things have been known to happen, although fortunately not too frequently. The majority of indexers seem content to check the page numbers on the proof with those in the "copy" or else to sample a few pages of the text at random and check off the indexable references in them with the page numbers set out in the index. A very thorough check, however, should be made whenever there has been a last minute repagination of the text.

## The Symbols

[This section applies mainly to book and periodical indexes, most of which continue to be printed by letterpress. It does not apply to the many index proofs which are now produced by other methods—such, for example, as by computer. The operators employed in computer processes are not printers and might fail to recognize proofreading marks and symbols.—Editor]

How should corrections be made? They should always be marked in ink. Certain symbols are used, which it is convenient to know. The 38 appearing on page 181 have been selected as the most likely ones to be required in correcting index proofs. They are extracted (by permission of the British Standards Institution) from the half-a-crown card B.S. 1219c: 1958—*Table of Symbols for Printers' and Authors' Proof Corrections*, which contains 64 symbols in all. For the modest outlay of six shillings one can obtain the table in a pamphlet with the same B.S. number and called: *Recommendations for Proof Correction and Copy Preparation*. This not only contains examples of corrected pages of print but even includes marks for clarifying and correcting mathematical copy. In the writer's opinion one or other of these B.S.I. publications is a "must" among the tools of the

British indexer's trade. American indexers can find comparable instructions in the *Manual of Style* issued by the University of Chicago Press (1949), pages 2 and 221.

British Standard (B.S. 1219) was first published in 1945, although some of its symbols must be nearly as old as printing itself, as signified by the use of the Greek letter "delta" and the Latin word "stet." The correction marks it contains are understood and followed by printers throughout the whole of Great Britain and America and in most other parts of the world, but the practice is materially different on the continent of Europe. The important question of promoting international agreement on this matter is being considered by a Committee of the International Organization for Standardization.

It will be observed in the table of symbols on the next page that every textual mark has its corresponding symbol to be used in the margin. The marginal marks can be used in either the left or the right margin, whichever is nearer the text to be corrected. Apart from minor differences in the symbols used, the following description of British practice would also apply to American usage.

No. 1 (/) is a marginal mark, placed after letters and words and certain punctuation marks to be inserted or substituted, to show that the correction is concluded. No. 2, the caret mark, is very common. It denotes that the letter(s) or word(s) indicated in the margin is/are to be inserted in the place marked. The new matter in the margin is followed by No. 1. No. 3 is probably the one most used. It is the Greek letter "delta" (though its origin might never be guessed from some writers' attempts to reproduce it), followed by No. 1, and is the deletion mark, signifying that the characters struck out in the text are to be erased. When these are in the middle of a word and the other letters must be closed up, then the close-up symbol (No. 16) must also be used both in the text and in the margin, as shown in No. 4. Similarly, where it is important that space should be left (as after deleting the hyphen in "no-one"), No. 18 marginal mark should follow No. 3 in the margin.

## Symbols And Marks For Correcting Index Proofs

| | Textual | Marginal | | Textual | Marginal | | Textual | Marginal |
|---|---|---|---|---|---|---|---|---|
| 1. | (none) | / | 14. | encircle damaged characters | ✗ | 27. | ‖ | ‖ |
| 2. | *[symbol]* | new matter followed by / | 15. | / through or *[symbol]* | *[symbol]* (e.g. *ÿ*) | 28. | = to straighten lines | = |
| 3. | Strike through what is to be deleted | *[symbol]* | 16. | linking characters | *[symbol]* | 29. | before first word | *n.p.* |
| 4. | Strike through and use mark No. 16 | *[symbol]* | 17. | / through ligature or diphthong | write out letters foll. by / | 30. | *[symbol]* | *run on* |
| 5. | ••• under what is to remain | *stet* | 18. | bet. words / bet. lines | # | 31. | / through or *[symbol]* | *[symbol]* |
| 6. | ‾ under characters to be altered | *ital.* | 19. | ( for lines / between words | *less* # | 32. | / or *[symbol]* | *[symbol]* |
| 7. | ～～～ as in No. 6 | *bold* | 20. | between words | *eq.* # | 33. | / or *[symbol]* | ⊙ |
| 8. | encircle characters to be altered | *rom.* | 21. | between characters or words | *trs.* | 34. | / or *[symbol]* | ⊙ |
| 9. | = as in No. 6 | *s.c.* | 22. | indicate position with | *centre* | 35. | / or *[symbol]* | ?/ |
| 10. | ≡ as in No. 6 | *caps.* | 23. | *[symbol]* | *[symbol]* | 36. | *[symbol]* or *[symbol]* | (/)/ |
| 11. | under initial letters ≡ under rest | *c. and s.c.* | 24. | *[symbol]* | *[symbol]* | 37. | *[symbol]* | /-/ |
| 12. | encircle characters to be altered | *l.c.* | 25. | [ | *take over* | 38. | *[symbol]* | /—/ |
| 13. | encircle characters to be altered | *w.f.* | 26. | ] | *take back* | | | |

No. 5. If one has crossed out something in the proof index and later wishes it to remain as printed, he puts dots (.....) under the characters to be retained and the word "stet" (Latin for "let it stand") in the margin opposite. No. 6 indicates the method of changing type into italics by means of an ordinary underline (_____) under the word or words in the text and placing ital. in the margin. No. 7 similarly demands changing to bold face type (note the wavy underline in the text), while from italics or bold face type to ordinary Roman needs No. 8. In this last case the characters affected in the text of the index are circled.

How to note changes to and from capitals (large or small) is shown in Nos. 9–12, two underlines being placed under characters to be put into small caps (s.c.) and three for large caps (caps). Note that "l.c." stands, not for "large capitals," but for "lower case" or ordinary type, as opposed to capitals. In this last case the characters affected are circled in the text. No. 13 "wrong font" (w.f.), which must also be encircled, will scarcely ever be found in the linotype or monotype in which our indexes are usually set.

No. 14 (×) is often required to get damaged type (to be encircled in the text) replaced. Here it is not always easy to distinguish between genuine damaged characters and cases where simply insufficient ink has been employed in that particular part of the proof, it being remembered that proofs are rarely printed with the same care as is the finished product. In such conditions duplicate proofs are invaluable because they can be compared to see if the character appears deformed in both. In cases of doubt the cross should be inserted in the margin. No. 15 is useful for the substitution or insertion of the apostrophe or quote marks or other characters to appear above the line. It can be used in conjunction with the delete mark, where an above-the-line character must come out.

No. 16 is the close-up symbol already mentioned in connection with No. 4. It should be used in both text and margin for deleting space between characters and for denoting ligatures (e.g., ffi) or diphthongs (e.g., æ or œ), the actual ligature or diphthong required being shown enclosed by the wings of the symbol in the margin. The reverse process is denoted by No. 17, the separate letters being written out in the margin, followed by No. 1. The provision of greater or less space, either between words or between lines, is demanded by Nos. 18–20.

Nos. 21–26 denote how matter is shifted; it sometimes makes for clarity in the case of transposition (No. 21) if small numerals are put in addition under misplaced words or letters to show the order in which they should appear. Thus, if confronted in the proof with such a jumble as "rebels the up," one could put "1" under "up," "2" under "the," and "3" under "rebels," with trs. in margin. Similarly, if presented with a mix-up like "tarpsnose," one could put figures under the letters to show that it should read "transpose." An alternative method, in either case, would be to strike out the offending passage and rewrite it correctly in the margin, ending with No. 1.

Nos. 23 and 24 are for moving matter to right or left, the former textual symbol being placed at the left of what is to be moved, the latter at the right. Nos. 25 and 26 are for taking over to next line or column or for taking back to the previous line or column. Nos. 27 and 28 are for correcting faulty alignment, the one, vertical, the second, horizontal; both are occasionally required in correcting index proofs.

The only occasions on which the writer uses No. 29 (n.p.) in an index is where new paragraphs seem indicated to break up an excessively long series of run-on subheadings. In such a case, bearing in mind what has already been said on the question of expense, one should use it rather in preparing the script than in correcting page proofs (see next paragraph). No. 30 is to obtain the reverse process. Nos. 31–38 denote how punctuation marks are inserted or substituted. Observe that the full stop and the colon are invariably encircled in the margin, the reason being probably that otherwise they might escape notice. The others, excepting Nos. 37 and 38, are followed by No. 1. No. 38, the one-em dash (frequently needed in an index), is inserted upon the writer's responsibility as no symbol for it appears in B.S. 1219.

As well as for correcting proof, the symbols on page 181 may also be employed in making amendments to one's own script. It might be mentioned that some occurred fairly frequently in the preparation of this chapter, which, elementary as it may be, may hopefully prove of practical use to indexers who are faced (perhaps for the first time) with the problem of correcting their proofs. Even experienced indexers (and consequently proofreaders) may find some of the hints contained in this chapter to be of value.

## The Practical Exercise

Page 186 represents the extract as it should look and as it was originally printed. On the next page certain deliberate mistakes have been made—far more than are ever likely to be found in a proof of this length. These are to be detected and put right. When this has been done, the result can be checked by turning to the corrected proof (page 202).

First, let us have a look for a moment at one or two points in the specimen index.

1. It is not easy to guess from the extract what kind of book is being indexed. Actually it is a recent *History of Trinidad and Tobago,* by Gertrude Carmichael (Alvin Redman Ltd.).
2. First entry. "1672 . . . 304." The dotted lines are simply a device for avoiding confusion between dates or other digits appearing at the end of the heading on the one hand and the page references on the other. Another method is to put such dates or digits in italics or parentheses, e.g., "captured by (1672)."
3. Notice the colon after "British Guiana." Whenever a heading is not followed immediately by page numbers, but only by subheadings, it is of the utmost importance that the punctuation after the heading should be a colon and not, as so often seen, a comma. See pp. 170–171.
4. Page references in italics. In this index these denote main topics. It seems preferable to employ bold type for this

purpose, but in this case the printers did not possess any bold type in the size used in the original index. The one example of bold type on the original proof is simply put there for the purpose of correction.

5. Bracketed descriptions (*Governor*, *Alcade*, etc.), it will be noticed, are printed in italics. This may be regarded as a whim of the writer and need not be followed by others. It was possibly adapted from the style used in theater programs (e.g., "Lady Macbeth (*wife of above*)")!

## EXTRACT FROM INDEX

## Extract from Index in Proof Form

Bridges, Sir Tobias, Tobago captured By, 1672 . . . 304

Bristol merchants' petition on Trinidad's laws, 92

British American Corporration, 288

British American Exchange Bank, 259

Britishand Foreign Bible Society, 200

British Guiana:
East Indian immigrants in, 214, 242, 243; immigration bounty system, 188;　See of (R.C.), 250

*British Trident,* repatration ship, 243

Broome, Sir F. Napier (*Governor,* 1891-7), 288, 301, 376

Brougham, Henry Peter (later Baron brougham), 89, 159, 242
— speech by, 1824 . . . 404

Brown, Alexander (*Lt.-Gov. of Tobago,* 1764-6), 306, 434.

Brown, Charlotte (Mrs. Burnley), 247

Brown, Frederick (Alcade), 160

Buchanan, R. T. (*Agent in New Pork*), 207

Buckingham, Richard Grenville, 3rd Duke oʒ (*Secretary of State*), 269-70

Buckley, Dr. James (*Vicar-Apostolic*), 128, 134, 149, 177, 250, 432

Buildings, *239-40, 247-8, 277-8*

Burnley, William (*Depositor-Gen.*), 93, 136, 145, 154, 170
— career of, 246-7; dele gate to England, 1832 . . . *161, 164-6;* estates of, *211, 239, 247;* immigration and, *206, 209-10, 247, 419-21;* Immigration and Agricultural Society chairman, *211;* Llanos's councillorship objected to by, *172-3;* opposed railway by, 1847 . . . 245; sales of estates stopped by, 127, slavery amelioration and, *122-4;* Survey Committeeman, 221; will of, *247*

Burnley, William F. (*estate owner*), 272

Burns, Captain, *188*

Bushe (*Alcade*), 160

Buxton, Sir Thomas Fowell ' Elephant " (*abolitionist*), 121, *164,* 242

## 14

# ARCHIVE INDEXING

LEONARD. C. JOHNSON

"What is all this fuss about a simple thing like indexing?" This querulous remark by the uninitiated, so often heard, sets the challenge of justification and explanation to all who care for the ready availability of sources of knowledge, a facility specially vital to those who pursue the important task of making history speak for today. It must be said immediately that though archives are important and fascinating from the viewpoint of antiquarianism, the archivist seeks to make his archives fulfill an additional role. Browning, in "A Death in the Desert," uses the striking figure of a "stick once fire from end to end, now ashes save the tip that holds a spark." The spark blown upon, runs back, spreads itself, and illumines the ashes into the original form of the stick. So does the live historian blow upon the records of past endeavors until the whole takes fire once more, illuminating the shape of massive undertakings and revealing the caliber of courageous men who took hold upon events and circumstances and molded them into revolutionary enterprises. Indeed "there were giants in the earth in those days," and we do well in these days to get the true measure of their stature.

Old books, papers, documents—of what use can they be in this thrusting, swiftly moving age when knowledge, one is told, is doubling itself every fifteen years? But knowledge has a habit of making cyclic re-eruptions, and often what seems to have passed into limbo takes fire and sets a new trail ablaze with live ideas. The modern active man, under the stress of high pressure activities, will sometimes, nay often, be rewarded by a pause and a backward look. But, endeavoring to keep astride of swift developments, how can he stay to unravel the story of the past? The historian can come to his aid with a compact resumé of past events and earlier notions that can still be inspirationally effective and serve a modern need astonishingly well.

But how may the historian, the researcher, find his way through the labyrinth of papers which may often obscure his path by their very multiplicity and complexity, or grievously tempt him to stray from his appointed purpose through the insidious but attractive serpent of serendipity? How blessed then is the guide of sound indexes which may proffer its services. But good indexes do not fall together casually or by chance; they are the work of assiduous, meticulous persons who know well that true indexing is no such simple task as our querulous critic surmises. Such work calls for special skills and a particularly sensitive insight into what is likely to be of real value, not only for today but also for tomorrow. A too scanty index is a tantalizing begetter of impatience; one overloaded is cumbersome, time-consuming, and befogging.

To make a good index is in fact to create an artificial "memory," so that memory may properly become the thing one can forget with, and so relax to pursue other tasks. Likewise both our contemporaries and posterity may be refreshed and instructed by the treasury of knowledge discovered and left on record.

The indexing of archives is especially rewarding, proving not only an instruction as to the past but also, by the very act of indexing, an appraisal of what is deemed vital for today and in the future. This has an important bearing upon business archives, for the business administrator may find that his records yield vital information relative to a current situation. Obviously everything cannot be indexed. Indeed the very omissions deliberately made may have their own significance. It is not easy, nor perhaps wise, to endeavor to separate the classification of archives from the actual indexing of them, for these are really two aspects of one act, classification being the broad outline and indexing the detailed notation.

When the researcher legitimately asks the archivist: "What have you got?" it is not sufficient to answer, "There is a card index which contains everything." A true picture of an archive collection cannot be gained by flipping over thousands of cards—an eye and nerve straining activity in any case. Neither can one answer the question properly by an overall reply of so broad a nature as to leave it wide open. One should be able to present a picture on a large canvas but one that is sufficiently detailed to enable the researcher to estimate easily whether he is justified in spending time and effort on the collection.

The writer contends that the best answer to the question is the creation of a summary register of archives, produced in loose-leaf form and arranged to suit the particular kind of archives in the repository. So far as British Transport archives are concerned, these take the form of records of over 1,000 railway companies, many joint committees, some 300 companies in the London Transport system, and river, canal, dock, and harbor undertakings, as well as about 300 miscellaneous companies including road and hotel undertakings. This factor must dictate the pattern for such a body embracing so many companies. The arrangement of company records must preserve the separate legal entity of each body from its inception until its extinction. This is a vital archive rule. The notation of relevant records will always therefore be made under the name of the particular company, and the loose leaves recording them will be inserted in this summary register in the strict alphabetical order of the names of the companies. Being in loose-leaf form this strict alphabetical sequence will never be disturbed by the acquisition of records of other companies from time to time. These company records form a separate section of the register.

Many other groups of archives are acquired that are not specifically company groups—governmental reports, returns, maps, plans, surveys, parliamentary records, general information, to name only a few. All are given their group titles, and the relevant loose leaves are filed in a separate section of the register, again in the strict alphabetical sequence of their title headings. In this summary index register, each company and miscellaneous group receives a classification sign in the form of letters, usually three, having some relationship with their title heading, i.e., LNW for the records of the London and North Western Railway Company; RAC for Reports and Accounts (in the miscellaneous section). The records are arranged in classes according to their fundamental nature: Minutes of the governing body, Capital stock and share registers, Locomotive and rolling stock records, Staff records, and many others, each class receiving a number which is common to all groups, and each separate item within the group having a "piece" number. Minutes, for example, of each company group are always Class 1 records. The full, and only, reference of the first L. & N.W. Rly. Minute Book is LNW./1/1, and this is its identity for all time. Here then is the Summary Index Register which presents the researcher with a ready answer to his question, "What have you got?" Incidentally a short legal history of each undertaking, and a description of each group of Miscellaneous Records has been written, and appears as the first page of the relevant records, and this gives the researcher important information as to the company or miscellaneous group to which he is referring.

For a more detailed description of the records he may now turn to the second loose-leaf register which answers two questions, the researcher's "What in particular?" and the office staff's "Where is it?" This detailed register comprises the record of each "piece" included in each class of each group. The loose leaves in this register are arranged in the strict alphabetical order of the denoting letters of each group, and the numerical sequence of each class, and within the class the chronological order of each "piece."

Thus to refer to LNW. 1 is to find the record of all the minutes of this company in strict date order. In addition, for the use of the staff, the filing location of every "piece" is inserted in a separate column, the precise location of a whole series of "pieces" appearing on a single page. The value, precision, and ease of reference of this system are considerable. If an alteration in location becomes necessary only one amendment is required in the register for perhaps a dozen or more "pieces." If on the other hand the location were recorded on index cards, several of which may have to be created for a single "piece," the task would become much more difficult and laborious, particularly as time will erode the memory of how many and what cards were created by the indexer, to say nothing of the passing of the indexer himself. In this second register, then, the researcher will have a detailed index of the quantity, nature, and date range of all the documents in the Repository, at the head office in London, and at the two branch offices in Edinburgh and York. The same system obtains for the branches as for the head office, duplicate sets of all the registers being kept by them and maintained up-to-date by a system of "amendment sheets" circulated between all three offices. Groups that are located at the branches are indicated by a red ink note at the top of each loose leaf—"Edinburgh" or "York."

A third index is necessary. This is in card index form and is termed the Comprehensive Card Index. This, for actual work, is probably the most important finding aid of all three. It is maintained on a name and subject basis, the references being to group, class, and "piece" number only. Each "piece" is indexed under as many headings as its nature and content warrant. No two persons can be certain of indexing in precisely the same manner, but in order to maintain the index with as much consistency as possible a few main guides have been formulated, conforming to general principles of indexing and to the particular requirements of the archive group. These guides are mounted at the index table that has been specially made to fit into a corner of the office with index cabinets on the two adjacent walls. The indexer, seated on a swivel chair, has access to all the index cabinets without rising from the chair and has ample accommodation on the table for the material being indexed. It should be mentioned that during the process of classification the notations are made on sheets which conform precisely to the actual loose leaves in the registers. This facilitates the typing of the original sheets considerably, making it much easier for the typist to transfer from replica to replica. In this process of classification, too, the archivist performing the task makes special reference to any particular matter in the "piece" which he has discovered during his examination of it and which he considers worth bringing out in the index. Indeed during every operation in the office all the staff are constantly alert for any item which may enrich the index. Indexing is, so to speak, "in the air" as a continuous atmosphere.

Only one comprehensive index is maintained, the tendency to multiply indexes being eschewed. If there are a number of indexes, almost certainly at times one of them will be forgotten during referencing. The very purpose of a true comprehensive index can be destroyed by multiplicity. The one exception made is the Library Index which is worked upon a different basis than that of the comprehensive index. Guide cards are liberally used in this latter index to break it up into swiftly ascertainable sections. The maintenance of this index is an essential part of the classification procedure. It is a strict rule that there shall be no hiatus in the process of dealing with an acquisition of archives. At no time may any of them be placed in abeyance waiting to be indexed at some more convenient time. Each piece must be taken through its whole routine and placed upon the shelves; then it can be forgotten, leaving the registers and the index to remember it for all time. By indexing thus, one's task never accumulates to become an almost impossible burden to dislodge. The time taken in maintaining the index is more than saved by its use when staff members are engaged upon the research and referencing necessary to run an archive repository successfully. Swift recourse to all relevant material is an absolute essential, and the comprehensive index is a vital part of the administrative system.

Thus, then, is the ready availability of all archives assured, by what may be termed a three-tier system of indexing, combining both classification and indexing as such, the one inseparable from the other. This combination of the loose-leaf registers with the card index has worked well, and to the writer seems capable of being applied, with perhaps suitable variations, to groups of archives of varying character.

The foregoing is chiefly a record of the system of indexing devised for one specific archival group, and manifestly other archive collections may require somewhat different methods. The nature of the collection will dictate the precise system best suited to make referencing swift and comprehensive. The basic principles should however remain constant, and at the risk of some repetition the following ones are cited as of special significance.

As most archive groups will expand by reason of continuing acquisitions, the index should be of a loose-leaf and/or card system so that it can be kept in strict order in perpetuity. Generally a card index is safer if used only by the staff, unless protected by a locking device to prevent the removal and subsequent misplacing of cards by a researcher. Although locking devices usually involve more work when new cards are inserted, some such device is essential if the researcher is to be allowed access. A loose-leaf register has its own built-in lock.

The danger of creating a number of indexes has already been emphasized, but there are considerable advantages in providing at least two. One should display the contents of the repository in broad outline, arranged in summary form. The researcher's time is valuable and he should be able swiftly to assess the value of the archive collection for his purpose. The form of such a summary has already been outlined. The writer has found that a condensed summary of this summary is invaluable for desk use when answering tentative inquiries requiring an immediate answer without recourse to the main summary.

The second index, in card form, should, without being laborious, be detailed and comprehensive, with every item in the repository indexed in as full a manner as the nature of the "piece" warrants and staff time allows. It must be stressed that although thorough indexing is itself time-consuming, it ultimately saves the user's time and greatly enhances the value of the archive collection.

Each of these indexes should be based upon the fundamental principle stressed by the late Sir Hilary Jenkinson in his valuable treatise *Archive Administration*: "the Archivist should class the Archives separately under the Administration which actually created them." This principle will require that each "piece" be indexed under its parent Administration, whether this be an individual or a corporate or other body, as well as under its subject heading. Some subjects will have varied names or aspects and it is proper to index all references to "pieces" under the best or most inclusive subject heading and make cross-reference cards for the other aspects, e.g.,

Armorial devices    [This should be main entry with subheading and all references.]

Coats of Arms    [This should be additional card bearing the cross reference:]

   *see* Armorial devices

Vague or unduly broad headings should be avoided. Alphabetical order should always be by the word-by-word method, i.e., *New cross* should come before *Newcastle*. Abbreviations should be filed as if the word were fully spelled, i.e., *St. Pancras* to be filed as *Saint Pancras*. The index should be compiled with a view to creating headings likely to be familiar now and, so far as one can judge, in the future. Emphasis should always be given to the main aspect of the reference by its position on the card so as to facilitate ready observation, i.e.,

*London and South Western Railway*
Exeter and Exmouth Railway opening

*not*

Opening of railway from Exeter to Exmouth

Perhaps some of the greatest problems arise when indexing the great miscellanea. Archives relating to specific individuals or corporate administrations are relatively easy to deal with, but large numbers of miscellaneous papers flow into a repository which may be termed orphans, having no defined parentage, but which may contain valuable information upon a variety of subjects. The best one can do is to endeavor to create groups of as many of a kind as can be collated and index them under such collation and as to subject. Those which cannot thus be brought together will remain as individual items under the general classless group "Miscellanea." The card index alone will be able to reveal them, for they will usually outgrow the possibility of being recorded individually in a register under the single heading "Miscellanea." In this respect a carefully created card index is of immense importance.

Of real significance is the manner of the production of the cards in the index. They should never be scribbled. This advice may sound superfluous, but the writer has seen with surprise many indexes scribbled in tiny handwriting. This vital finding aid should never test the sight or the patience of the user. Cards must be clearly legible and are best typed, but when additions have to be made by pen they must be scrupulously neat and clear. The use of upper-case lettering is not advocated, since it has been demonstrated that capitals are less easily read than lowercase lettering.

Surely the index is not something that the user should have to bother over. It should be a device to provide clear, immediate, and stimulating references. Indexing must not therefore be thought of as a task to push on to the junior and most inexperienced staff member; it is a work that calls for special skill, insight, and mature knowledge.

Indeed the index is the touchstone of the quality of the archive collection.

# SOLUTIONS TO EXERCISES

*Chapter 3 Exercise 1 ( page 56)*

| WORD-BY-WORD | | LETTER-BY-LETTER | |
|---|---|---|---|
| Man, Alfred B. | (4) | Man, Alfred B. | (4) |
| Man, Isle of | (21) | *Man and Superman* | (19) |
| *Man and Superman* | (19) | Man and wife | (10) |
| Man and wife | (10) | Man-eating tigers | (6) |
| *Man for All Seasons, A* | (1) | *Man for All Seasons, A* | (1) |
| Man Friday | (2) | Man Friday | (2) |
| *Man from Blankley's, The* | (25) | *Man from Blankley's, The* | (25) |
| *Man in the Iron Mask, The* | (11) | Mangoes | (9) |
| *Man Who was Thursday, The* | (3) | Manhattan | (23) |
| Man-eating tigers | (6) | *Man in the Iron Mask, The* | (11) |
| Mangoes | (9) | Man, Isle of | (21) |
| Manhattan | (23) | Manitoba | (8) |
| Manitoba | (8) | Manjrekar, V. | (24) |
| Manjrekar, V. | (24) | Man-made fiber | (14) |
| Man-made fiber | (14) | Mann & Co. | (5) |
| Mann & Co. | (5) | Manning, Director of | |
| Manning, Director of | | R.A.F. | (15) |
| R.A.F. | (15) | Manningtree | (17) |
| Manningtree | (17) | Man-of-war | (7) |
| Manorbier | (20) | Manorbier | (20) |
| Manpower | (18) | Manpower | (18) |
| Mansfield | (12) | Mansfield | (12) |
| Mansfield, Earl of | (13) | Mansfield, Earl of | (13) |
| *Mansfield Park* | (16) | *Mansfield Park* | (16) |
| Man-of-war | (7) | Mantua | (22) |
| Mantua | (22) | *Man Who was Thursday, The* | (3) |
| Manzanares | (26) | Manzanares | (26) |

## Chapter 3 Exercise 2 (page 57)

| WORD-BY-WORD | | LETTER-BY-LETTER | |
|---|---|---|---|
| South, Rev. Robert | (1) | South, Rev. Robert | (1) |
| South African War, the | (8) | South African War, the | (8) |
| South America | (7) | Southall, borough of | (16) |
| South Carolina | (19) | South America | (7) |
| South Georgia | (18) | Southampton | (15) |
| South Pole, the | (9) | South Carolina | (19) |
| South Sea Bubble, the | (12) | Southcott, Joanna, her box | (10) |
| *South Wind* | (21) | South-East Asia Command | (3) |
| Southall, borough of | (16) | Southend-on-Sea | (14) |
| Southampton | (15) | Southern, Victor R. | (6) |
| Southcott, Joanna, her box | (10) | Southern Cross, the | (20) |
| South-East Asia Command | (3) | Southern Railway, the | (5) |
| Southend-on-Sea | (14) | Southey, Robert | (2) |
| Southern, Victor R. | (6) | South Georgia | (18) |
| Southern Cross, the | (20) | South Pole, the | (9) |
| Southern Railway, the | (5) | Southport | (13) |
| Southey, Robert | (2) | South Sea Bubble, the | (12) |
| Southport | (13) | Southsea Pier | (11) |
| Southsea Pier | (11) | Southwark, borough of | (17) |
| Southwark, borough of | (17) | South-West African Mandate | (4) |
| South-West African Mandate | (4) | *South Wind* | (21) |

## Suggested Answers to Exercise, Chapter 4 (page 74)

1. Chen Yi, Marshal
2. Attlee, 1st Earl
3. Mahapol, Nai Sawat
4. de Valera, President Eamon
5. le Gallais, Hugo
6. Horn, Gen. Carl von
7. de la Mare, Walter
8. Del Bo, Rinaldo
9. Paul I, H.M. King of the Hellenes
10. Manzur Qadir
11. Rooy, Pieter van
12. Pachero Batlle, César
13. Attlee, Rt. Hon. Clement Richard, *see* Attlee, 1st Earl
14. van Straubenzee, William R.
15. Clerc, Gen. François de
16. Southwark, Bishop of, *see* Stockwood, Rt. Rev. A. Mervyn,
   *and*
   Stockwood, Rt. Rev. A. Mervyn
17. Jawad, Hashim
18. Swaran Singh, Sardar
19. Salazar, Dr. Antonio de Oliveira
20. Arias Salgado, Don Gabriel
21. Ormsby-Gore, Rt. Hon. W. David

22. Gonvorath, Kham Sing
23. Suleiman bin Dato Abdul Rahman, Inche
    Rahman, Inche Suleiman bin Dato Abdul, *see* Suleiman
24. Tin Maung, Thakim
25. La Pira, Giorgio
26. Gokhale, Gopal Krishna
27. Abdul Aziz ibn Hassan, Sheikh
    Hassan, Sheikh Abdul Aziz ibn, *see* Abdul

Answer to Proof-Correcting Exercise, Chapter *13* (*pp.* 186–187)

## EXTRACT FROM INDEX

*p.c.*

Bridges, Sir Tobias, Tobago captured By, 1672 . . . 304

*w.f.*

Bristol merchants' petition on Trinidad's laws, 92
British American Corporation, 288
British American Exchange Bank, 259
British and Foreign Bible Society, 200
British Guiana:
East Indian immigrants in, 214, 242, 243; immigration bounty system, 188; See of (R.C.), 250

*less #*

British Trident, repatriation ship, 243
Broome, Sir F Napier (*Governor,* 1891-7), 288, 301, 376
Brougham, Henry Peter (later Baron Brougham), 89, 159, 242
— speech by, 1824 . . . 404

*cap.*

Brown, Alexander (*Lt.-Gov. of Tobago,* 1764-6), 306, 434.
Brown, Charlotte (Mrs. Burnley), 247

*ital.*

Brown, Frederick (*Alcade*), 160
Buchanan, R. T. (*Agent in New York*), 207

Buckingham, Richard Grenville, 3rd Duke of (*Secretary of State*), 269-70
Buckley, Dr. James (*Vicar-Apostolic*), 128, 134, 149, 177, 250, 432
Buildings, 239-40, 247-8, 277-8
Burnley, William (*Depositor-Gen.*), 93, 136, 145, 154, 170
— career of, 246-7; delegate to England, 1832 . . . 161, *164-6;* estates of, *211,* 239, 247; immigration and, *206, 209-10,* 247, *419-21;* Immigration and Agricultural Society chairman, *211;* Llanos's councillorship objected to by, *172-3;* opposed railway by, 1847 . . . 245; sales of estates stopped by, 127; slavery amelioration and, *122-4;* Survey Committeeman, 221; will of, 247

*trs.*

*;/*

Burnley, William F. (*estate owner*), 272
Burns, Captain, *188*
Bushe (*Alcade*), 160
Buxton, Sir Thomas Fowell "Elephant" (*abolitionist*), 121, *164,* 242

Brodie, Rev. G., 272

# SELECTED BIBLIOGRAPHY

American Standards Association. *American Standard Basic Criteria for Indexes*. New York, 1959. 11 pp.

Anon. *Preparation of Manuscripts and Correction of Proofs*. Cambridge, Eng., 1951.

British Standards Institution. *Alphabetical Arrangement* (B.S. 1749: 1951), 12 pp.

- - - *Recommendations for the Preparation of Indexes*. (B.S. 3700: 1964), 31 pp.

Carey, Gordon V. *Making an Index*. 3d ed. Cambridge, Eng., 1963. 13 pp.

Clarke, Archibald L. *Manual of Practical Indexing*. 2d ed. London, 1933.

Collison, Robert L. *Indexes and Indexing*. 2d ed. 1959. 200 pp.

- - - *Indexing Books*. 1962. 96 pp.

Friedman, Harry A. *Newspaper Indexing*. Milwaukee, Wis., 1942. 261 pp.

Harris, Eleanor T. *A Guide for the Preparation of Indexes*. Santa Monica, Calif., 1965. 36 pp.

Hines, Theodore C., and Jessica L. Harris. *Computer Filing of Index, Bibliographic, and Catalog Entries*. Newark, N.J., 1966. 126 pp.

Jonker, Frederick. *Indexing Theory, Indexing Methods and Search Devices*. New York, 1964. 124 pp.

Metcalfe, John W. *Alphabetical Subject Indication of Information*. Rutgers, N.J., 1965. 148 pp.

- - - *Information Indexing and Subject Cataloguing: Alphabetical, Classified, Coordinate, Mechanical*. New York, 1957, 338 pp.

Spiker, Sina. *Indexing Your Book.* 2d ed. Madison, Wis., 1954. 28 pp.

Taube, Mortimer. *Studies in Coordinate Indexing.* 3 vols. Bethesda, Md., 1953, 1954, 1956.

Walsh, John W. T. *The Indexing of Books and Periodicals.* London, 1930. 118 pp.

Weeks, Bertha M. *How to File and Index.* Rev. ed. New York, 1961. 306 pp.

Wheatley, Henry Benjamin. *How to Make an Index.* London, 1902. 236 pp.

Wheeler, Martha T. *Indexing: Principles, Rules, and Examples.* 5th ed. New York, 1957. 78 pp.

To these books should be added chapters on indexing in various books of literary studies, including Sir Edward Cook's "The Art of Indexing" from his *Literary Recreations* (1918) and Stephen Leacock's "Index: There Is No Index" from his *My Remarkable Uncle* (1942); also a number of important specialist articles in *The Indexer* and occasional contributions to library and other periodicals. Among the latter are five by John Askling: "Confusion Worse Confounded" in *The California Librarian*, Vol. 13, No. 2 (1951), 91, 92; "Indexer Goes to Work" in *ibid.*, Vol. 13, No. 1 (1951), 30–32; "What Is an Index" in *ibid.*, Vol. 12, No. 3 (1951), 159, 160; "What Makes an Indexer Tick" in *ibid.*, Vol. 12, No. 4 (1951), 211–213; and "Words at Work" in *Library Journal*, Vol. 78 (1953), 1879–1882.

The American indexer can turn with confidence to *A Manual of Style*, published by The University of Chicago Press (11th ed. [1949], 12th printing), pp. 178–187 and 211–213.

Some publishing houses issue their own house guides on this subject, a very useful one being by Messrs. Faber & Faber, entitled *Notes for Authors on the Preparation of MSS for the Printer.* These do not as a rule deal specifically with the editing of indexes.

# INDEX

Compiled by the Editor

This index has been deliberately made somewhat fuller than what might have been deemed adequate for a book with a different title.

Allusions to "Index," "Indexing," and "Indexer" occur on almost every page of the text; the index entries to them have been reduced to a minimum of those that would not be looked for under some other heading.

Page references 14–39 are printed in *italics* for the convenience of solvers of the Exercise on page 39. References in **bold type** indicate that the item has a whole section devoted to it.

*Bis* after a reference number denotes that the item is alluded to *twice* quite separately on the same page of the text; q. stands for quoted; *q.v.* for *quod vide* (which see).

The alphabetical arrangement is word-by-word.

Abbreviations, alphabetical arrangement of
in archive index, 195
compound, **51**
simple, **47–49**
symbols for, 151
Abdul Rahman, Tenku, 61
Abdul Razak bin Hussein, 67
Abstracts, 2, 96, 97, 116–117
L'Académie Française, dictionary of, *18*
Accents and alphabetical order, **41–42**
Acharya, Vinoba Bhave, 68
Acknowledgments, **8**
Adjectives and adverbs as key words, 119
*Adult Education* (journal), index to, 102
Advertisements, indexing of, *16*, *26*
African tribal surnames, 65, 66, 70
Afridi, Monawar Khan, 67
Agencies, indexing, 6

"Al" as name prefix, how indexed, 65
Allusions, hidden, abstruse, or esoteric, 91
Alphabetical arrangement, **40–57**, **73–74**, 112–113
advantage of, 40, 113
in archive indexes, 195
beginnings of, *21–22*
classification and, *17–18*, 81
editing attention to, **169**
in legal indexes, 164–165
practical exercises for, **56–57**, **198–199**
resistance to, *17–18*
of subheadings, 95
of surnames, 69–70
*See also* Letter-by-letter alphabetizing; *and* Word-by-word alphabetizing
*Alphabetical Arrangement* (B.S. 1749: 1951), 40
compound headings rule in, 50, 52 *bis*